T0030944

AFTER MATH

Life in Post-Roe America

Edited by Elizabeth G. Hines

SHE WRITES PRESS

Published 2022
Printed in the United States of America
Print ISBN: 978-1-64742-601-9
E-ISBN: 978-1-64742-602-6
Library of Congress Control Number: 2022916923

For information, address:
She Writes Press
1569 Solano Ave #546
Berkeley, CA 94707

Interior Design by Tabitha Lahr

She Writes Press is a division of SparkPoint Studio, LLC.

For my family
—JM, AGHM, SIHM, SCHM, CJ and MH—
who make everything possible

And for
Rachael Wells,
who fought bravely and rightly
for the most important thing in life:
Love.

"The way to right wrongs is to turn
the light of truth upon them."
—IDA B. WELLS

CONTENTS

Introduction
Elizabeth G. Hines xiii

Raising a Daughter in a Post-*Roe* World
Jessica Valenti 1

My First Abortion Story
Alyson Palmer 5

**Controlling Bodies and Subverting
Democracy: How *Dobbs* Is an Attack on Us All**
The Reverend Dr. Liz Theoharis 11

As Goes Mississippi, So Goes America
Linda Villarosa 21

So They All Just Lied?
Heather Cox Richardson 27

**Biden Must Do More to Protect
Abortion Rights**
Alyssa Milano 33

**The Abortion Stories We Didn't Tell: How
Decades of Silence Left Us Unprepared for
the Post-*Roe* Fight**
Rebecca Traister 37

Get Real
Jennifer Baumgardner 45

Our Body Is Our Own
Ruby Sales. 53

Facing Higher Teen Pregnancy and Maternal
Mortality Rates, Black Women Will Largely
Bear the Brunt of Abortion Limits
Cecilia Lenzen 60

"*Roe* Was the Floor"
*A Q&A with Elizabeth Estrada, National
Latina Institute for Reproductive Justice* 68

How the Supreme Court Decision Limiting
Abortion Access Will Harm the Economy and
Women's Financial Well-being
Michele Estrin Gilman. 77

To Imagine a World without *Roe*,
Look to Kentucky
April Simpson and Melissa Hellmann. 82

Society Makes a Choice Before Any of Us Can
Soraya Chemaly 89

No, Justice Alito, Reproductive Justice *Is*
in the Constitution
Michele Goodwin 95

Reproductive Justice Advocates Can't
Afford to Ignore How Abortion Bans
Affect Asian Americans
Jenn Fang 101

Abortion Is a Disability Issue
Robyn Powell 110

Collateral Damage
Ann Craig 116

For Indigenous Peoples, Abortion Is a
Religious Right
Abaki Beck and Rosalyn Lapier 126

Not All Religious People Oppose Abortion
Sarah Seltzer 131

The Beautiful Scream
Lisa Sharon Harper 136

"Every Single One of Them Responded in Tears"
*A Q&A with Robin Marty, West Alabama
Women's Center* 142

Clinic
Alissa Quart 152

My Trip to Texas Gave Me a Glimpse Into
the Post-*Roe* Future
Rosa Valderrama 157

The Privilege of Hope: Working in Partnership
with Young People
Tamara Marzouk 162

A Letter to My Mother
(and Like-Minded Individuals)
Mina Row 167

My Daughter's First Pro-Choice Protest
Rob Galvin 171

Rewriting the Rules: A Pharmacist's Fight to
Make Medication Abortion Accessible to All
Dr. Jessica Nouhavandi 175

A Black Abortion Provider's Perspective
on Post-*Roe* America
Bria Peacock, MD 180

For the Patients
Cordelia Orbach 184

"No Amount of Preparation Could Have
Minimized the Devastation"
*A Q&A with Margaret Chapman Pomponio,
WV Free* 189

Abuse, Discrimination, Exclusion: Transgender Men Explain Domino Effect of Losing Reproductive Care Post-*Roe*
Orion Rummler 198

My Story
Amy Ferris 204

Pushing Back on the Politics of Hypocrisy
Sonali Kolhatkar 208

Is Violence the Last Gasp of Patriarchy?
Gloria Feldt 213

We Need a Post-*Roe* Strategy for the Long Haul. Global Feminists Offer a Blueprint
Yifat Susskind 218

6 Ways to Fight for Abortion Rights After *Roe*
Katha Pollitt 223

Girding Our Loins: A Spiritual Survival Guide for the Battle Ahead
Chaplain Lizzie Berne DeGear, PhD 229

How to Help 237
Acknowledgments 238
About the Editor 241

INTRODUCTION

ELIZABETH G. HINES

There are moments in history that change you.

I was born in 1975, two years after the Supreme Court affirmed *Roe*. At forty-seven years old, I have no lived experience of a time when abortion was illegal. My childhood, teenage years, and adulthood have all unfolded in a legal context that, at least theoretically, protected the right of every individual to determine the fate of their own body with regard to pregnancy, and, thus, the direction of their own life.

That freedom—even as it was constantly challenged and unevenly accessed—formed the fundamental, empowering assumption of my own young life: that my body was mine to own; that the decision about how, whether, and when I might become, or remain, pregnant was a decision I alone would get to make. As luck would have it, I grew up and grew a family of my own in a time and place when the laws of this land protected my right to decide how my life would unfold. It was a privilege to be a member of one of the generations that benefited so profoundly from the rights *Roe* won us—though it is worth acknowledging how many of us took those rights for granted, given how little we chose to understand about what life might look like once they were gone.

Now, the days of blithely assuming that the impossible could never happen are officially over. After nearly fifty years as settled constitutional law, the federally protected right to an abortion in America is a thing of the past. For the first time in the history of this nation, the Supreme Court has rescinded an affirmed human right, and the cost of that upheaval is being felt both practically and energetically by individuals across this nation.

Let's not hesitate to say it: For those of us who believe in the right of all human beings to determine their own destiny, the overturning of *Roe* is a devastating loss. And the people who will pay the highest price are those who already have the least resources, and the most racial- and identity-based discrimination stacked against them. What may qualify as an inconvenience for well-resourced people (the need to travel; the cost of the procedure) can be life-altering for those already struggling to get by. As a Black woman, I see and feel this clearly as stories roll in about women and girls—many of whom look much like me and my daughters—who have either been denied care or forced to travel hundreds of miles to access it.

On the night the draft of the Supreme Court's decision on *Dobbs v. Jackson Women's Health Organization* leaked to the press, it became clear to me that life as I knew it was about to be upended. I was furious and sad, and then filled with dread over what to tell my daughters about their loss of equality and bodily autonomy.

I wasn't the only one reeling. My phone was alight with text messages from mothers—and fathers—who, in similar states of anger and sadness, were all wrestling with the same question: *What do we do now?*

There are certainly many answers to that question. One thing we must do now is give money to on-the-ground providers doing the critical work of supporting access to reproductive health services (and buying this book helps in that regard, as a portion of all proceeds will go to fund the work of reproductive health organizations in the US). Another thing we must do is get out in the streets and raise our voices in the name of equality and justice. And for those of us who can, we must VOTE. Now more than ever, state and local elections matter, so we must do everything we can to protect the right to vote—and use that right—every single chance we get.

There is something else, too—and the book you're holding in your hands is part of my own answer to the question. We can *tell our stories.* Share our truths. Lift up our voices and make clear our perspectives on what this loss of rights means to us—now, and for the future. Perhaps because so many of us could never imagine a world in which this right would be taken away, we have not, in the aggregate, been very good at sharing and listening to stories about what it is like to end a pregnancy in this country, or what the lack of access to reproductive health services means for the lives of people seeking care. But silence is no longer an option. Lives, as you will learn in these pages, are at stake. If we hope to claim a future that gets closer again to recognizing the authority of women and pregnant people to make critical decisions about their own bodies, then we must raise our voices everywhere, and use our outrage to build collective action for change.

This book exists to help put words to the various experiences people have had in accessing abortion care through the years, and to provide a snapshot of this particular moment in history—the moment when the loss of *Roe* finally became real. The essays you will read in this book are the narratives of people who have had abortions themselves, and they are the testimony of experts who work in the field. They are the words of theologians, lawyers, activists, historians, journalists, and everyday people with informed perspectives on how lack of abortion access will impact the lives of Black and brown and Asian and Indigenous and queer and trans and disabled and poor and young people across this country. They don't all agree on every aspect of the work that lies ahead of us, or on how we got here, but they have lent their voices to this collection because, like me, they believe in the power of stories to change lives. To spur action. To inspire hope. To move mountains. And in the name of equality and justice, that is exactly what we plan to do.

I did not begin the year 2022 imagining that I would end it by releasing a book on reproductive rights. But what I said at the beginning of this introduction is true: there are indeed moments in history that change you, and this moment, this attack on our freedom, has provided me with a necessary reminder that we all have a role to play in fighting for the future we want to see. I hope you will read each of these essays, or even just a few, and be moved to take action in support of the human dignity of all those who can become pregnant. A better future lies in all of our hands.

RAISING A DAUGHTER IN
A POST-*ROE* WORLD

JESSICA VALENTI

M y daughter feels invincible. At eleven years old, she is all confidence and smiles, optimism, and resilience.

She doesn't know about the ten-year-old rape victim in Ohio who was impregnated and forced to leave the state to get an abortion. She has no idea that conservatives on television and in politics called the child's story a lie—or that when forced to admit its veracity, those same people doubled down and said it was fine for a tiny body to be forced into pregnancy.

She can't imagine that would ever be her.

She doesn't read the news or intently watch Twitter; she doesn't realize that as she happily goes to school and camp, plays video games and hangs out with friends, that girls only slightly older than her are being denied birth control at their local pharmacies. She is blissfully ignorant of the women in hospitals bleeding for days on end, unable to get a doctor to treat their miscarriage because their doomed fetus still has a heartbeat. She doesn't know that a woman whose boyfriend hurts her might be brought to court by his family should she decide she doesn't want a child to bind her to the abuse for the rest of her life.

She plays and she laughs; she hugs me and runs off.

When I asked my daughter how she was feeling about *Roe* being overturned—she knows all about abortion and the Supreme Court decision (if she's old enough to be forced into pregnancy, she's old enough to know about abortion)—she responded that she wasn't nervous at all. When I pushed further, asking her why she wasn't afraid, she gave an answer that nearly broke me: "I know you'd never let anything bad happen to me."

I feel grateful that I have raised a child with enough love and safety that she believes I can protect her from anything. But I wondered, in that moment, if I had done her a disservice, giving her a sense of untouchability that no girl or woman has.

Yes, she will likely be okay. We live in New York and have enough money to bring her out of the state, or even out of the country, if that ever becomes necessary. Despite her pre-teendom, she still sees me, as so many little girls do their mothers, as superhero-like. She has watched me make a fuss and raise hell when I need to; listened to me yell at boys on a playground for pushing her; read the emails I sent to school administrators, tearing into them for allowing gross sexism in the classroom.

Her eyes light up when I am at my most furious over an injustice—she loves to watch me set something right. I have let her believe that there is nothing I can't do.

I can't help but feel like a liar. Because there are so many things I cannot shield her from, and I am terrified at what she might think of me once she inevitably realizes that disappointing truth.

Will she hate me when a man calls out to her on the street because I'm not there to help her? Will she ever see me the same way once she realizes that so much of my power is for show?

She doesn't know that her life and the way she wants to live it are already limited. There are colleges she can't go to because they're in states that would let her die rather than allow her to end a pregnancy. Places she will never be safe because their laws don't see her as a full person. The ability to move freely, to travel, and to choose where life may take her has already been stolen from her.

If abortion is outlawed nationally—a horror that is a lot more possible than most of America would like to believe—it would happen in 2024, the year my daughter turns fourteen years old. She would be a teenager, and at her most vulnerable to be impacted by a countrywide ban.

If that were to happen, my gut instinct would be to leave the US. How could I raise her in a place that thinks so little of her, a place where there is no safe haven? But to do so would be to abandon all I have worked for, and all the others who can't just pack up and drive off. How could I possibly meet her gaze then?

I want her to feel protected, always. But I also know she needs to build the ability to fight for herself, to stand up and yell out even when I am gone. My heart is just broken that I can't leave her with a world where she doesn't have to do so very often.

I know I haven't failed. It's parental instinct to try to make our children feel more safe in the world, despite its dangerous reality. I know she will forgive me for making her feel too safe in a country that is anything but for women. But the truth is that I'm not sure I will ever forgive myself.

MY FIRST ABORTION STORY

ALYSON PALMER

M y mom crept quietly up the stairs after the Senior Dance and locked herself in the bathroom. She told me her hands were trembling as she set down the glass bottles as silently as she could. Disturbing her foster mother, Mrs. Scott, at this hour meant a lashing. My mom stripped off her clothes and lay down in the tub. One after another, she pried off the tops of five bottles of Coca-Cola. Spreading her legs high against the wall of tiles it was her job to scrub twice a day until they gleamed, she poured each bottle of Coke into the throbbing spot between her legs, desperately hoping that what she'd heard was true, that this was how to prevent a pregnancy.

It all happened so fast. She was with that popular boy in the front seat of his car after the dance, where they'd been so admired for their grace circling the floor. She'd never thought he'd notice her, yet here they were on their first date and the night had been perfect. When he leaned over, she let him kiss her and kiss her. She melted in his arms. She kissed him back with all the yearning she'd stored in her heart for sixteen lonely years. Suddenly, she was pinned under the steering wheel and he was hurting her. She didn't know what to do. After it ended, they were silent. He drove her home. He wouldn't look at her and she was ashamed. He mumbled an apology, saying she was so beautiful he couldn't help himself.

She knew she'd done something wrong. She felt the familiar bewilderment that came with a Mrs. Scott whipping for an infraction she couldn't understand. Remembering what some girls had whispered in school, she slid into the pantry and scooped up an armful of Coca-Cola bottles from the wooden cases Mrs. Scott kept in front of her bourbon.

My mom told me that what she remembered most was sticky liquid everywhere, stinging her torn skin as it filled her and the tub, and hating herself for ruining one of the best nights of her life.

My mother's mother drove off on tour with her drummer husband when my mom was four years old, leaving my mother behind. Their neighbor, Mrs. Scott, took her in and raised her to follow orders, clean, and never step out of line, or she'd be beaten back. Mrs. Scott never mentioned bodies changing or sex—other than to say it was dirty, that doing it before marriage ruined a girl forever, and that it was a barely tolerable necessity to keep a husband, as she'd dutifully done until her own husband died. He'd shot off his head in the kitchen. My mother, then age thirteen, had found him and called the police, and she was the one who had cleaned up the blood and tissue after they took the body away. Mrs. Scott had stayed drunk upstairs in the tub she slept in so the bats wouldn't get her. She'd finally come down the next day to a spotless kitchen and the news her husband had died.

The only two things my mother taught me about sex were that women weren't ruined by it, but that they had much to fear from it. Women inflamed men to passions they couldn't control. I know that her intention was to teach me to stay vigilant, be cautious, dress carefully. But what I learned from her words was that I must be an avenging warrior defending downtrodden women and that a woman must be in charge, always, of whether to keep a pregnancy or not.

My mother's life continued to be dark. Before she turned forty, she developed an unknown condition that made her tremble, fogged her brilliant mind, and made her skin burn from the inside. After years of tests and dozens of doctors, a neurologist declared her condition was close enough to multiple sclerosis to call it that. Neither of her husbands cared enough to stick around to the end of her story. Living with her worsening condition, deepening depression, and painful lack of self-esteem convinced me as a teen that I would never have children to watch me wither when that disease inevitably claimed me too.

September 11 changed that. On a solo trip a month after the devastation of my downtown, I was compelled to try and make sense of the world any place where stars vastly outnumbered people. With no one in sight for miles in every direction, I sat in a lengthening shadow between my rented convertible and a giant cactus and had an epiphany that I felt reverberate across the windswept desert. I understood I had to create more love for the world. I would work for fairness, play for harmony, and pour so much love into another being it would spill over and help heal broken spirits.

From the minute she was born, she has. She's a radiant miracle whose heart is vast and deep. Her gaze can soothe like a moonbeam.

When our daughter was around three, my beloved partner, Tony, and I were moving furniture in our cozy New York apartment. As we carried a sofa up the stairs, I was drained of energy so suddenly that I was struck with panic. Was this the moment? Had my mother's disease finally caught up with me? Had I tempted fate with my joy?

It was my toddler who told me I had a baby growing in my tummy. Her dad agreed. As much as I denied the possibility, I went to the OB/GYN, who confirmed it.

With one child, I had gotten lucky. Wasn't two pushing it? Our lives were going so well. We could still work and play and had plenty of amazing time with our baby girl now that she was old enough to reason and read. Could we afford the mental-physical-emotional-financial toll of growing another being?

I discussed every aspect with Tony and my best friends, including how fortunate I was to have the freedom to choose what the hell to do, how grateful I was to live in America. Making that decision was the most adult I'd ever felt, connecting with the wisdom of women through the centuries. This precious commitment was sacred. Whatever I decided would be holy and would honor the loving, trusting God who'd created in me the ability to make this choice.

I'd had an abortion with Tony about a decade before when a condom broke. That was two years into our relationship and there wasn't even a question. There was no way two hard-partying musicians should be parents while on tour. I'd seen the results.

Over the next ten days, Tony and I made peace with the idea that we were no longer going to play two-on-one zone defense. With another kid, we'd be playing man-on-man. Tony was elated.

I was terrified but proud of my resolve when I went in for an ultrasound. The excitement bubbled up while we chatted and Dr. Meredith prepared the wand. I caught my breath when she suddenly grew quiet. Something was wrong.

The egg sac was there and growing, but it appeared empty. The embryo had disappeared. I couldn't understand the situation completely at first, just that what was growing wasn't right, and I should get the remaining tissue out or it could turn septic and make me sick. I needed to wash my insides out with a sea of liquid, whether I wanted to or not. I thought of my mom and her overflowing soda pop. Here I thought I was striding boldly in a new direction, but I was still following her path.

Dr. Meredith gave me a pill. Hours later, I took another. She said it would take a few hours to expel the tissue, but nothing happened. I had tickets to see the Broadway musical of my favorite book, *The Color Purple* by Alice Walker. After eight hours of not even a stomach gurgle, I went ahead to the theater. I bought a giant bag of peanut M&M's for solace. Fantasia, Danielle, Renee, and the rest of the amazing cast enthralled me, and I left my buzzing brain behind as I was swept into the familiar story of abused but indomitable Celie.

As the climax built before intermission, something shifted. I was seized with a cramp so strong I bent forward. As the curtain came down for intermission, I ran to the nearest bathroom.

I was stunned by how much poured out of me. The cramps kept squeezing and more blood of my sweet possibility gushed free. After some time, people pounded on the door, but there was nothing I could do. I tried to yell my apology through the door, but just had to wait for the abortion to finish its cycle, like the giant coin-op washing machines at the cleaner. The bells signaling the end of intermission began to ding. I felt drained and light-headed and my pants were crimson with blood, but damn it this was Broadway and the show must go on. I put on fresh pads, tied my hoodie around my waist, mumbled apologies as I passed the line of infuriated seniors lined up outside the door, ripped open the M&M's, and sat crying through the second half of the show.

I cried for the loss of Junior, as I'd come to think of him. I cried because clearly it wasn't his time to come to me yet—he had to wait on his pink and gold cloud for the right moment—but I missed him already. I cried because I was scared I might never stop bleeding. I cried because Celie in *The*

Color Purple had been abused and belittled and was devoid of self-esteem, but the women around her raised her up. Their fierce love and patient understanding gave her the support to do anything, including believe in herself. I cried because in another circumstance, maybe my mom could have uncovered her own Celie and soared. I cried because I was relieved. I cried because I felt guilty for being relieved. I cried because it was a perfect perfectly horrible amazing awful fortunate moment I knew I'd never forget. I felt alive, weeping and popping peanut M&M's with a best friend who understood, and my whole life spread out like a pick-your-own-adventure story once more, pages shifting with infinite possibilities.

A year later, I got pregnant intentionally and had a beautiful son who brought with him the pink and gold of his waiting cloud. I am a warrior, forged in the Herculean journey of my own deeds. Boldly in control of my destiny, I have become the mother I prayed I could be—the mother I wish my mom could have known.

ALYSON PALMER is the singing songwriter, producer, and teaching artist best known for her long career in the award-winning indie rock trio BETTY. As an equality activist, she is a Stonewall Ambassador, an Arts Envoy with the US State Department, and a proud member of the ERA coalition. In 2016, Aly founded 1@1 Productions to create effective arts actions for social justice, including the global "1@1 Minute for Women's Equality" and "Women Take the Stage," the multi-performer virtual concert and rally held on the centennial of the 19th Amendment to increase voting by and for women. @alyzonpalmer

CONTROLLING BODIES AND SUBVERTING DEMOCRACY: HOW *DOBBS* IS AN ATTACK ON US ALL

THE REVEREND DR. LIZ THEOHARIS

When I was the age that my daughter is now, my favorite sweatshirt had the words "Choice, Choice, Choice, Choice" in rainbow letters across its front. My mom got me that sweatshirt at a 1989 rally in response to *Webster v. Reproductive Health Services*. In that case, the Supreme Court upheld a Missouri law restricting the use of state funds and facilities for abortion, an early attempt to eat away at *Roe v. Wade*. And though many adults in the Wisconsin neighborhood where I grew up thought that message inappropriate for a thirteen-year-old, I wore it proudly. Even then, I understood that it spoke not just to a person's right to an abortion, but also to the respect and dignity that should be afforded every human being.

Since then, it has become increasingly clear that our society does not confer rights and dignity on *we the people*—as seen in the slashing of school food programs, the denial of Medicaid expansion in states that need it most, attacks on Black, Brown, and Native bodies by the police and border patrol, as well as the Supreme Court's recent decisions to put fossil fuel companies ahead of the rest of us, put guns above kids, and deny sovereignty to Indigenous people and tribes, while failing to protect our voting rights and ending the constitutional right to abortion.

For millions of us, the *Dobbs v. Jackson* decision on abortion means that life in America has just grown distinctly more dangerous. The seismic aftershocks of that ruling are already being felt across the country: twenty-two states have laws or constitutional amendments on the books now poised to severely limit access to abortion or ban it outright. Even before the Supremes issued their decision, states with more restrictive abortion laws had higher maternal mortality and infant mortality rates. Now, experts are predicting at least a 21 percent increase in pregnancy-related deaths across the country.

As is always the case with public health crises in America—the only industrialized country without some form of universal health care—it's the poor who will suffer the most. Survey data shows that nearly 50 percent of women who seek abortions live under the federal poverty line, while many more hover precariously above it. In states that limit or ban abortion, poor women and others will now face an immediate threat of heightened health complications, as well as the long-term damage associated with abortion restrictions.

Indeed, data collected by economists in the decades after *Roe v. Wade* indicates that the greater the limits on abortion, the more poverty for parents and the less education for their children. Worse yet, the thirteen states that had trigger laws designed to outlaw abortion in the event of a *Roe* reversal were already among the poorest in the country. Now, poor people in poor states will be on the punishing speartip of our post-*Roe* world.

While the Supreme Court's grim decision means more pain and hardship for women, as well as transgender and gender nonconforming people, it signals even more: the validation of a half-century-old strategy by Christian nationalists to remake the very fabric of this nation. For the businessmen, pastors, and politicians who laid the foundations for the *Dobbs* ruling, this was never just about abortion.

The multi-decade campaign to reverse *Roe v. Wade* has always been about building a political movement to seize and wield political power. For decades, it's championed a vision of "family values" grounded in the nuclear family and a version of community life meant to tightly control sex and sexuality, while sanctioning attacks on women and LGBTQIA people. Thanks to its militant and disciplined fight to bring down *Roe*, this Christian nationalist movement has positioned itself to advance a full-spectrum extremist agenda that is not only patriarchal and sexist but also racist, anti-poor, and anti-democratic. Consider the *Dobbs* decision the crown jewel in a power-building strategy years in the making. Consider it as well the coronation of a movement ready to flex its power in ever larger, more violent, and more audacious ways.

With that context, bear in mind that, in his concurring opinion, Justice Clarence Thomas suggested that the *Dobbs* decision gives the Supreme Court legal precedent to strike down other previously settled landmark civil rights jurisprudence, including *Griswold v. Connecticut* (access to contraception), *Lawrence v. Texas* (protection of same-sex relationships), and *Obergefell v. Hodges* (protection of same-sex marriage). Whether or not these fundamental protections ultimately fall, the Supreme Court majority's justification for *Dobbs* certainly raises the possibility that any due-process rights not guaranteed by and included in the Constitution before the passage of the 14th Amendment in 1868 could be called into question.

The Christian nationalist movement long ago identified control of the Supreme Court as decisive for its agenda of rolling back all the twentieth-century progressive reforms from the New Deal of the 1930s through the Great Society of the 1960s. Less than a week after the *Dobbs* decision, in fact, that court overturned *Massachusetts v. EPA*, the 2007 ruling that set a precedent when it came to the government's ability to regulate greenhouse gas emissions by polluting industries. May Boeve, head of the environmental group 350.org, put it this way:

> Overturning Roe v. Wade *means the Supreme Court isn't just coming for abortion—they're coming for the right to privacy and other legal precedents that* Roe *rests on, even the United States government's ability to tackle the climate crisis.*

To fully grasp the meaning of this moment, it's important to recognize just how inextricably the assault on abortion is connected to a larger urge: to assault democracy itself, including the rights of citizens to vote and to have decent health care and housing, a public-school education, living wages, and a clean environment. And it's no less important to grasp just how a movement of Christian nationalists used the issue of abortion to begin rolling back the hard-won gains of the Second Reconstruction era of the 1950s and 1960s and achieve political power that found its clearest and most extreme expression in the Trump years and has no interest in turning back now.

ABORTION AND THE ARCHITECTURE OF A MOVEMENT

Throughout American history, a current of anti-abortion sentiment, especially on religious grounds, has been apparent. Some traditional Roman Catholics, for instance, long resisted the advance of abortion rights, including a church-led dissent during the Great Depression, when economic disaster doubled the number of abortions (then still illegal in every state). Some rank-and-file evangelicals were also against it in the pre-*Roe* years, their opposition baked into a theological and moral understanding of life and death that ran deeper than politics.

Before all this, however, abortion was legal in this country. As a scholar of the subject has explained, in the 1800s, "Protestant clergy were notably resistant to denouncing abortion—they feared losing congregants if they came out against the common practice." In fact, the Victorian-era campaign to make abortion illegal was driven as much by physicians and the American Medical Association, then intent on exerting its professional power over midwives (mainly women who regularly and safely carried out abortions), as it was by the Catholic Church.

Moreover, even in the middle decades of the twentieth century, anti-abortionism was not a consensus position in evangelical Protestantism. For example, the Southern Baptist Convention, evangelicalism's most significant denomination, took moderate positions on abortion in the 1950s and 1960s, while leading Baptist pastors and theologians rarely preached or wrote on the issue. In fact, a 1970 poll by the Baptist Sunday School Board found that "70 percent of Southern Baptist pastors supported abortion to protect the mental or physical health of the mother, 64 percent supported abortion in cases of fetal deformity, and 71 percent in cases of rape."

So what changed for those who became the power brokers of a more extremist America? For one thing, the fight for the right to abortion in the years leading up to *Roe* was deeply intertwined with an upsurge of progressive gender, racial, and class politics. At the time, the Black freedom struggle was breaking the iron grip of Jim Crow in the South, as well as segregation and discrimination across the country; new movements of women and LGBTQIA people were fighting for expanded legal protection, while challenging the bounds of repressive gender and sexual norms; the increasingly unpopular war in Vietnam had catalyzed a robust antiwar movement; organized labor retained a tenuous but important seat at the economic bargaining table; and new movements of the poor were forcing Washington to turn once again to the issues of poverty and economic inequality.

For a group of reactionary clergy and well-funded right-wing political activists, the essence of what it was to be American seemed under attack. Well-known figures like Phyllis Schlafly and Paul Weyrich, who would later found the Moral Majority (alongside Jerry Falwell, Sr.), began decrying the supposed rising threat of communism and the dissolution of American capitalism, as well as what they saw as the rupture of the nuclear family and of white Christian community life through forced desegregation. (Note that Jerry Falwell didn't preach his first anti-abortion sermon until six years after the *Roe* decision.)

Such leaders would form the core of what came to be called the "New Right." They began working closely with influential Christian pastors and the apostles of neoliberal economics to build a new political movement that could "take back the country." Katherine Stewart, author of *The Power Worshippers: Inside the Dangerous Rise of Religious Nationalism*, often cites this Paul Weyrich quote about the movement's goals:

> *We are radicals who want to change the existing power structure. We are not conservatives in the sense that conservative means accepting the status quo. We want change—we are the forces of change.*

Indeed, what united these reactionaries above all else was their opposition to desegregation. Later, they would conveniently change their origin story from overt racism to a more palatable anti-abortion, anti-choice struggle. As historian Randall Balmer put it: "Opposition to abortion, therefore, was a godsend for leaders of the Religious Right because it allowed them to distract attention from the real genesis of their movement: defense of racial segregation in evangelical institutions."

Many of the movement's leaders first converged around their fear that segregated Christian schools would be stripped of public vouchers. As Balmer points out, however, they soon recognized that championing racial segregation was not a winning strategy when it came to building a movement with a mass base. So they looked elsewhere. What they discovered was that, in the wake of the *Roe* decision, a dislike of legalized abortion had unsettled some Protestant and Catholic evangelicals. In other words, these operatives didn't actually manufacture a growing evangelical hostility to abortion, but they did harness and encourage it as a political vehicle for radical change.

Looking back in the wake of the recent *Dobbs* decision obliterating *Roe v. Wade*, Katherine Stewart put it this way:

> *Abortion turned out to be the critical unifying issue for two fundamentally political reasons. First, it brought together conservative Catholics who supplied much of the intellectual leadership of the movement with conservative Protestants and evangelicals. Second, by tying abortion to the perceived social ills of the age—the sexual revolution, the civil rights movement, and women's liberation—the issue became a focal point for the anxieties about social change welling up from the base.*

What this movement and its allies also discovered was that they could build and exert tremendous power through a long-term political strategy that initially focused on southern elections and then their ability to take over the courts, including most recently the Supreme Court. Abortion became just one potent weapon in an arsenal whose impact we're feeling in a devastating fashion today.

A FUSION MOVEMENT FROM BELOW?

As Reverend William Barber, co-chair of the Poor People's Campaign, has pointed out, check out a map of the states in this country that have banned abortion and you'll find that you're dealing with the same legislators and courts denying voting rights, refusing to raise municipal minimum wages, and failing to protect immigrants, LGBTQIA people, and the planet itself. As the Economic Policy Institute described the situation after Supreme Court justice Samuel Alito's leaked draft opinion on abortion hit the news in May:

> *It is no coincidence that the states that will ban abortion first are also largely the states with the lowest minimum wages, states less likely to have expanded Medicaid, states more likely to be anti-union 'Right-to-Work' states, and states with higher-than-average incarceration rates. . . . Environments in which abortion is legal and accessible have lower rates of teen first births and marriages. Abortion legalization has also been associated with reduced maternal mortality for Black women. The ability to delay having a child has been found to translate to significantly increased wages and labor earnings, especially among Black women, as well as increased likelihood of educational attainment.*

Indeed, the right to abortion should be considered a bellwether issue when judging the health of American democracy, one that guarantees equal protection under the law for everyone. Fortunately, the most recent Supreme Court rulings, including *Dobbs*, are being met with growing resistance and organizing. Just weeks ago, thousands upon thousands of us came together on Pennsylvania Avenue for a Mass Poor People and Low Wage Worker's Assembly and Moral March on Washington and to the Polls. On the very day of the *Dobbs* decision, protests against that ruling, including acts of nonviolent civil disobedience, began, and they have been growing ever since.

In a similar fashion, striking numbers of us have begun mobilizing against gun violence and the climate crisis. At this moment as well, we seem to be witnessing the rise of a new labor movement, with workers already organizing at Starbucks, Dollar General stores, and Walmart, among other places. The Christian nationalist movement relies on a divide-and-conquer strategy and single-issue organizing. A pro-democracy and justice movement must resist that approach.

As a Christian theologian and pastor myself, I've been deeply disturbed by the growth of the Christian nationalist movement. We would do well, however, to heed their focus and fury. Its leaders were very clear about how necessary it was, if they were ever to gain real power in this country, to build a national political movement. In response, the 140 million poor and low-wealth Americans, pro-choice and pro-earth activists, and those of us concerned about the future of our democracy must do the same, building a moral movement from below. And such a movement must not be afraid of power, but ready to fight for it. Only then can we truly begin to reconstruct this country from the bottom up.

AS GOES MISSISSIPPI,
SO GOES AMERICA

LINDA VILLAROSA

In 2018, my mother and I traveled to Iuka, in the northeast part of Mississippi, where her mother was born at the tail end of the 19th century. While listening to the audiobook of Isabel Wilkerson's *The Warmth of Other Suns*, we drove through miles and miles of raw beauty: lush trees bursting with green, red dirt, and a stillness interrupted only by the occasional warm gust of wind. In the mid-1920s, as a teenager, my mother's mother became the last of her seven brothers and sisters to escape both the poverty and racial terrorism described in Wilkerson's work and travel up north to Chicago, a land of milk and honey for so many during the Great Migration of the past century.

Beneath the miles and miles of natural beauty my mother and I drove through, poverty and racial terrorism, most recently in the form of reproductive injustice, lie just beneath the surface. Mississippi is the Blackest of all the states (outside of the District of Columbia): nearly 40 percent of residents are African American. It has the highest rate of poverty, with nearly 20 percent of Mississippians barely hanging on, and the lowest life expectancy, 74 years compared to the national average, 78.8 years. The state ranks dead last in the health of women and children as well; it has the nation's highest rates of infant and child mortality and among the worst in maternal death and near death.

On June 24, 2022, when the Supreme Court ruled on *Dobbs v. Jackson Women's Health Organization*, closing the last abortion clinic in Mississippi and ending the constitutional right to abortion nationwide, posts in my social media feed predicted a return to the bad old days pre-*Roe v. Wade*. But like most Black women, I didn't join in the *Handmaid's Tale* chorus of woe and screams of injustice. *Dobbs* was never just about abortion, as people in Mississippi, all over the South, and throughout Black America have long understood. It is about control over our bodies, which we have never fully had, making the *Dobbs* decision less apocalyptic and more business-as-usual.

Without a doubt, what happened to us in the past in the US, with its deep roots in slavery and anti-Blackness, has a direct throughline to today, to the *Dobbs* decision.

Beginning over 400 years ago, forced labor had a double meaning for us: Enslaved Black women's reproductive abilities raised the fortunes of the South and the rest of the country by providing generations of unpaid workers who labored under a system of inhumane violence. Our bodies—bought, sold, and bartered—created additional wealth for the slave-holding South. And Black parents also lacked the autonomy to protect their children, who could be ripped away based on the false idea that Black people had a superhuman pain tolerance, including to unimaginable emotional pain.

After the end of slavery, when our fertility became not a

commodity but a burden, that too was torn away. In one of the most egregious examples, again in Mississippi, the voting rights activist Fannie Lou Hamer was given a hysterectomy without her consent in 1961 when undergoing removal of a uterine tumor by a white physician. The practice of being sterilized, including during unrelated surgery, grew so common among poor Black women in the South that it came to be known as a "Mississippi appendectomy."

In the neighboring state of Alabama, in the summer of 1973, two young Black girls, Minnie Lee and Mary Alice Relf, ages fourteen and twelve, were taken from their home in Montgomery, cut open, and sterilized against their will and without the informed consent of their parents by a physician working in a federally funded clinic. Eventually their case, *Relf v. Weinberger*, would change the course of history: the lawsuit filed on their behalf helped reveal that more than 100,000 mostly Black, Latina, and Indigenous women had been sterilized under US government programs over decades. But the practice was most sinister and longstanding in the South. When cotton was no longer king in states like Mississippi and Alabama and mechanization caused agricultural jobs in the fields to dry up, poor Black folks crowded into southern cities like Montgomery and Jackson. This influx of rural Blacks made people whose ancestors had carried the economy of the South on their backs a liability that needed to be controlled and, far too often, eliminated.

Black women have been screaming into the wind that reproductive rights are about more than abortion in earnest since 1994. That year, a group of Black women rejected the narrow framework of "reproductive rights" as overly focused on "choice" (aka abortion) and coined the term reproductive justice (RJ). The framework they laid out nearly thirty years ago is simple and matters more than ever today. The tenets of that framework, as defined by the RJ organization SisterSong, are: "The human right to maintain personal bodily autonomy, to have children, not have children, and to parent the children we choose to have in safe and sustainable communities."

Several years ago, I asked Loretta Ross, one of the foremothers of the movement and a founder of SisterSong, to explain what RJ meant. She used her personal story as a blueprint for what can go wrong when a Black woman enters the reproductive care system and explained that the trauma she experienced earlier in her life provided the groundwork for her activism and thinking. At age eleven, Ross was raped by a stranger while on a Girl Scout outing in Central Texas. Three years later, in 1968, she became pregnant through incest, before abortion was legal. She decided to give up her baby for adoption, but the hospital brought her son to her and she changed her mind. Because she chose to keep her child, she lost her scholarship to Radcliffe College. As a nineteen-year-old student at Howard University, she used the Dalkon Shield to avoid getting pregnant again. At twenty-three, her fallopian tubes ruptured and she was sterilized. "That was my reproductive career, beginning to end," Ross told me, letting out a hoarse belly laugh. "As you can see, I'm emblematic of what goes wrong in a poor Black girl's life."

In my family, something different happened: Rather than end my grandmother's life, an illegal abortion might have actually saved it. Though she was able to escape the racial terror of Mississippi, she couldn't outrun poverty. In the late 1920s, she met my grandfather—who had traveled north from another town in Mississippi—at a dance on the south side of Chicago. They married and had my mother in 1930, my uncle the following year. Just as they got a toehold in the Promised Land up north, the Great Depression struck, and Black people were hit hardest and longest. My grandmother became pregnant again in 1932—around the same time grandfather lost his job as a hotel bellhop, along with all the other Black men who were fired and replaced by white men. They knew they could not afford another child, so my grandmother begged her physician to perform an abortion. She also made the choice to have her tubes tied to avoid future pregnancies, an unusual decision in those days.

My grandparents survived the Depression. My grandmother eventually got her beauty license and worked in a hair salon, while my grandfather found a job as a Pullman porter. In the 1940s, my grandmother earned her real estate license and helped my grandfather purchase a building—despite discriminatory housing practices, including redlining, which has been so well-documented in Chicago and other cities. Eventually, my grandparents were able to send my mother to college and graduate school, thus cementing our family legacy of education, homeownership, and survival.

Without the reproductive freedoms my grandmother fought to secure—to have a baby, to not have a baby, and to raise children outside of poverty and danger—abortion rights alone are meaningless. If those who have now limited our human right to end pregnancy actually cared about the lives of children in Mississippi, or anywhere else in this country, they would prove to us that the Black lives they have made their business to control do matter. They could invest deeply in Black children by preventing them from being routinely imprisoned or murdered by law enforcement. They could ensure that our communities have access to clean air and water, fresh food, and safe housing. They could support our right to vote without governmental interference. Finally, they could advocate for equitable health care, free from the poisons of discrimination and bias.

LINDA VILLAROSA is a contributing writer at *The New York Times Magazine* and a professor at the Craig Newmark Graduate School of Journalism, with a joint appointment at the City College of New York. Her book *Under the Skin: The Hidden Toll of Racism on American Lives and on the Health of Our Nation* was published in 2022.

SO THEY ALL JUST LIED?

HEATHER COX RICHARDSON

On the evening of Monday, May 2, 2022, a draft of the Supreme Court's then-pending decision on Dobbs v. Jackson Women's Health Organization was leaked to the public—setting off a firestorm of media coverage regarding the court's by then clear intention to overturn Roe v. Wade. The following essay, posted by historian Heather Cox Richardson on May 3, 2022, offered readers of her Letters to An American newsletter important context for the moment in time we then found ourselves in, with the federally protected right to abortion on the brink of extinction and the legitimacy of the Supreme Court a hot topic among many.

—EH

In 1985, President Ronald Reagan's team made a conscious effort to bring evangelicals and social conservatives into the voting base of the Republican Party. The Republicans' tax cuts and deregulation had not created the prosperity party leaders had promised, and they were keenly aware that their policies might well not survive the upcoming 1986 midterm elections. To find new voters, they turned to religious groups that had previously shunned politics.

"Traditional Republican business groups can provide the resources," political operative Grover Norquist explained, "but these groups can provide the votes." To keep that base riled up, the Republican Party swung behind efforts to take away women's constitutional right to abortion, which the Supreme Court had recognized by a vote of 7–2 in its 1973 *Roe v. Wade* decision and then reaffirmed in 1992 in *Planned Parenthood v. Casey*.

Although even as recently as last week only about 28 percent of Americans wanted *Roe v. Wade* overturned, Republicans continued to promise their base that they would see that decision destroyed. Indeed, the recognition that evangelical voters would turn out to win a Supreme Court seat might have been one of the reasons then–Senate majority leader Mitch McConnell refused to hold hearings for then-president Barack Obama's nominee for the Supreme Court, Merrick Garland. Leaving that seat empty was a tangible prize to turn those voters out behind Donald Trump, whose personal history of divorces and sexual assault was not necessarily attractive to evangelicals, in 2016.

But, politically, the Republicans could not actually do what they promised: not only is *Roe v. Wade* popular, but also it recognizes a constitutional right that Americans have assumed for almost fifty years. The Supreme Court has never taken away a constitutional right, and politicians rightly feared what would happen if they attacked that fundamental right.

Last night, a leaked draft of a Supreme Court decision, written by Justice Samuel Alito, revealed that the court likely intends to overturn *Roe v. Wade*, taking away a woman's constitutional right to reproductive choice. In the decision,

Alito declared that what Americans want doesn't matter: "We cannot allow our decisions to be affected by any extraneous influences such as concern about the public's reaction to our work," he wrote.

The dog has caught the car.

Democrats are outraged; so are the many Republican voters who dismissed Democratic alarms about the anti-abortion justices Trump was putting on the court because they believed Republican assurances that the Supreme Court justices nominated by Republican presidents and confirmed with Republican votes would honor precedent and leave *Roe v. Wade* alone. Today, clips of nomination hearings circulated in which Justices Amy Coney Barrett, Brett Kavanaugh, Neil Gorsuch, Clarence Thomas, and even Samuel Alito—the presumed majority in favor of overturning *Roe v. Wade*—assured the members of the Senate Judiciary Committee that they considered *Roe v. Wade* and the 1992 *Planned Parenthood v. Casey* decision upholding *Roe* settled law and had no agenda to challenge them.

Those statements were made under oath by those seeking confirmation to our highest judicial body, and they now appear to have been misleading, at best. In addition, the decision itself is full of right-wing talking points and such poor history that historians have spent the day explaining the actual history of abortion in the United States. This sloppiness suggests that the decision—should it be handed down in its current state—is politically motivated. And in a Pew poll conducted in February, 84 percent of Americans said they believed that justices should not bring their political views into their decision-making.

Senator Susan Collins (R-ME) and Senator Lisa Murkowski (R-AK) provided key votes for Trump's nominees and are now on the defensive. Collins publicly defended her votes for both Gorsuch and Kavanaugh around the time of their confirmation, saying she did not believe they would overturn *Roe*. She noted that Gorsuch was a coauthor of "a whole book" on the importance of precedent, and that she had "full confidence" that Kavanaugh would not try to overturn *Roe*. Murkowski voted to confirm Gorsuch and Barrett.

Collins today said: "If this leaked draft opinion is the final decision and this reporting is accurate, it would be completely inconsistent with what Justice Gorsuch and Justice Kavanaugh said in their hearings and in our meetings in my office." Like Collins, Murkowski noted that the final decision could change, but "if it goes in the direction that this leaked copy has indicated, I will just tell you that it rocks my confidence in the court right now." The draft is not going in "the direction that I believed that the court would take based on statements that have been made about *Roe* being settled and being precedent."

Washington Post columnist Jennifer Rubin suggested that the Senate Judiciary Committee should hold hearings on whether the justices lied in their confirmation hearings, and call Senators Collins and Murkowski as witnesses.

This apparent shift from what they had promised is a searing blow at the legitimacy of the Supreme Court, which was already staggering under the reality that three of the current justices were nominated by Donald Trump, who lost the popular vote and then tried to destroy our democracy; two were nominated by George W. Bush, who also lost the popular vote in his first term; and one other is married to someone who supported the January 6 insurrection and yet refused to recuse himself from at least one case in which she might be implicated.

Today, Republicans tried to turn this story into one about the leak of the draft document, which is indeed a rare occurrence (although not unprecedented), rather than the decision itself. Senate minority leader Mitch McConnell (R-KY) blamed the leaker for attacking the legitimacy of the court, although McConnell's refusal in 2016 to hold hearings for Obama's Supreme Court nominee on the grounds that eight months was too close to an election to confirm a justice before shoving Barrett through in October 2020 when balloting was already underway arguably did more to undermine the court's legitimacy. Echoing him, one commentator said the draft leak was worse than the January 6 insurrection.

But while McConnell and the right wing are implying that a liberal justice's office leaked the draft, there is no evidence either way. Observers note, in fact, that the leak would help the right wing more than the dissenters, since it would likely lock in votes. Those trying to blame the liberal justices did not comment on an apparent leak from Chief Justice Roberts's office that suggested he wanted a more moderate decision. Jennifer Rubin suggested calling the bluff of those blaming the liberal justices: she proposed agreeing that whichever office leaked the draft ought to recuse from the final decision.

Republican politicians have largely stayed silent on the draft decision itself today, but the reaction of Nevada Republican Adam Laxalt, who is running for Senate, suggested the pretzel Republican politicians are going to tie themselves into in order to play to the base without alienating the majority. Laxalt issued a statement on Twitter that said the leaked draft represented a "historic victory for the sanctity of life," but also said that since abortion is legal in Nevada, "no matter the Court's ultimate decision on *Roe*, it is currently settled law in our state."

Democrats, though, are not only defending the constitutional right recognized by *Roe v. Wade* but also calling attention to the draft's statement that the Fourteenth Amendment under which the Supreme Court has protected civil rights since the 1950s can cover only rights that are "deeply rooted in this Nation's history and tradition."

It seems likely that the right-wing justices, who are demonstrating their radicalism by overturning a fifty-year precedent, are prepared to undermine a wide range of constitutional rights on the grounds—however inaccurate—that those rights are not deeply rooted in the justices' own version of this nation's history and tradition.

Protesters turned out in front of the Supreme Court and across the country today vowing that women will not go backward. As actress Ashley Nicole Black tweeted: "There's a particular slap to the face of being told we can vote for abortion rights, by the court that gutted voting rights."

Reprinted from Letters from an American, *by permission of Heather Cox Richardson.*

HEATHER COX RICHARDSON is an American historian and Professor of History at Boston College and the author, most recently, of *How the South Won the Civil War: Oligarchy, Democracy, and the Continuing Fight for the Soul of America.* Her newsletter, *Letters from an American*, is published nightly on Facebook and Substack and is read by over a million people a day. It chronicles current events in the larger context of American history.

BIDEN MUST DO MORE TO PROTECT ABORTION RIGHTS

ALYSSA MILANO

Just about a half-century ago, things were looking up for women in America. In 1972, Congress passed the Equal Rights Amendment, which upon ratification by 38 states would enshrine constitutional equality for all of us. And then, in 1973, the Supreme Court ensured women would have the freedom to control our own bodies when it affirmed the right to abortion in *Roe v. Wade*. But now, fifty years later, women have lost our most basic protections and our very bodily autonomy because of the cowardice of our government and a decades-long campaign by the extreme right to control and commodify us. We can't let it stand—and the good news is that we don't have to, if the president will simply grow a pair of ovaries and act.

For generations of women like me, who were born around or after the time of the *Roe* decision, the right to abortion has been a given—even if access to abortion care has not. Most people don't know this—Justice Alito certainly doesn't seem to—but abortion was legal in our nation until the late 1800s, when elected extremists criminalized our ability to control our bodies. In the decades between this dangerous government overreach and the *Roe* decision (and in the decades since), women fiercely fought for basic rights of American existence: the right to vote, to work, to earn equal wages, and to decide if, how, and when we want to have children—rights which men have always enjoyed and profited from. Recently, I made a short video with NowThis which covers the history of abortion in America and explores the long and passionate efforts of women who worked ceaselessly for these protections. I hope you will watch and share it with everyone you know.

The Supreme Court and radicalized anti-woman officials in state governments are working to set women back more than 150 years, to those first anti-abortion laws in the 1800s. As soon as *Roe* fell, dozens of states moved to criminalize abortion. Many states now even prohibit ending a pregnancy in cases of rape or incest. In the first four months of 2022 alone, at least 546 abortion restrictions were introduced. Thirty-seven have been enacted in ten states so far this year. Eighty-six abortion bans were introduced in thirty-one states, with six—Arizona, Florida, Idaho, Kentucky, Oklahoma, and Wyoming—enacting them. Oklahoma's new law is the strictest, prohibiting almost all abortions starting at fertilization and weaponizing vigilante citizens to sue health care providers or anyone who "aids or abets" an abortion. And it gets worse: some politicians are trying to prevent abortions even when the mother's life is in danger. And somehow, these people still have the temerity to call themselves pro-life.

The Equal Rights Amendment states that "Equality of rights under the law shall not be denied or abridged by the United States or by any state on account of sex." In 2020, Virginia became the 38th state to ratify this Amendment, and yet it still isn't in the Constitution. Why? Because Congress put an arbitrary and cynical poison pill into the preamble of the Amendment limiting the time frame for its ratification, and anti-woman forces have used this language to block its adoption. However, leading constitutional scholars contend that the preamble is not part of the Amendment and not binding language, and that the ERA is properly ratified.

Is there anything more obviously discriminatory on account of sex than denying access to health care to only one sex? Right now, President Biden could pressure the National Archivist to publish the ERA, making it the 28th Amendment to the Constitution. We need to be ensuring women have EQUAL rights enshrined in the Constitution, not reducing or rolling back rights they already have. It is mind-boggling that instead he is following in the footsteps of Donald Trump. Women helped elect President Biden. Now, we're calling in our investment. He must do everything in his power to enshrine our rights as Americans and to our own bodies in the Constitution.

If you think the radical right will stop at abortion, you need to think again. As late as 1974, women in parts of the country couldn't get a credit card without their husband's permission. The right to acquire and use birth control is at risk. Title IX protections may be dismantled as the anti-woman right continues its attacks against trans women and trans children. And despite their incessant lies that the dismantling of *Roe* will simply allow states to determine what rights women have inside their own borders, those extremists are clearly working toward a national abortion ban.

Women have always been lesser in this nation. This fact is the antithesis of everything we are taught the United States stands for, and yet it has persisted for centuries. And unless President Biden or Congress fixes it, right now, it's about to get so much worse for us. I hope you'll watch my video on abortion, gather every bit of patriotism and courage you have, and join me in loudly demanding that President Biden protect the women who put him where he is by pushing to enshrine equal rights in our Constitution right this second. Tomorrow might be too late.

To watch Alyssa's video on the history of abortion in America, please visit: https://bit.ly/MilanoRoe

This piece is published by permission of the author and Vox Media, LLC. It was originally published on May 31, 2022 at https://www.thedailybeast.com /alyssa-milano-biden-must-do-more-to-protect-abortion-rights?ref=home.

ALYSSA MILANO is an actor, producer, activist, and *New York Times* best-selling author. She hosts and produces the podcast *Sorry Not Sorry*, which is also the name of her most recent book. She is on the ERA Coalition's Advisory Council and is the ACLU's Ambassador for Reproductive Rights.

THE ABORTION STORIES WE DIDN'T TELL: HOW DECADES OF SILENCE LEFT US UNPREPARED FOR THE POST-*ROE* FIGHT

REBECCA TRAISTER

In 2004, I covered a pro-choice gathering of over a million people in Washington, DC, called the March for Women's Lives. I was twenty-eight, and most of the speakers and celebrities onstage were much older, many of them veterans of the second-wave feminist movement. I watched with dismay as Whoopi Goldberg waved a coat hanger at the crowd and chided its younger members: "You understand me, young women under thirty? This is what we used!"

At the time, I wrote that Goldberg "was scolding a generation for its privilege" and thereby committing movement malpractice by alienating young people, blaming them for not knowing about a world into which they were not born. I still think it was bad form; after all, if people in the crowd didn't know about pre-*Roe* abortion practices, half the blame surely lay with the elders who had not told them and who had perhaps evinced less curiosity about what abortion care was like during *Roe*. But I've also thought a lot in the years since that gathering about how *everyone* should have talked about it more: about pre-*Roe* abortions, *Roe*-era abortions—about abortions, period. Now, in a post-*Roe* world, I feel even greater frustration at the decades wasted, the millions of stories that did not get told, not just onstage in front of big crowds but in families, social circles, and civic and religious contexts.

The smug incuriosity of the mainstream American media has played a role in the absence of abortion stories. So has the caginess of the Democratic Party, which is loath to even say the word *abortion* and has too frequently pushed the framework of "safe, legal, and rare," casting abortion as some dolorous outcome rather than a cornerstone of reproductive health care, economic and familial well-being, and, therefore, equality itself. Even the reproductive rights movement has kept a distance from nuanced, varied stories of abortion, leaving us with a dearth of understanding, an absence of sympathy, a cluelessness about the conditions under *Roe* and the state of things going forward.

Ironically, it has been young people—like those Goldberg was haranguing in 2004—who have pushed for a more explicit conversation about what abortion is, how people experience it, and why it is a tool for liberation. But their work has really just begun. They are playing catch-up after decades of silence and curtailed narratives.

I haven't had an abortion, but when I was pregnant with my second child, the erosion of access across the country led me to seek out stories from my own family. It's not that these stories were kept from me; my mother, for example, had always been open about having had an abortion. But even as a thirty-nine-year-old who had been writing about gender, power, and abortion for more than a decade at that point, I'd never pursued the why or how.

I was startled by the sheer variety of abortion experiences revealed by just a couple of questions: My married grandmother had conceived accidentally and hadn't had the money for a child during the Depression. Her daughter, my aunt, unable to get the abortion she'd needed as a teen in the early '60s, had given birth to my cousin. That same aunt had two more children and four subsequent abortions, she told me, because she wasn't good at using birth control; one was administered with a knitting needle, and another was performed by Robert Spencer, the Pennsylvania doctor who provided illegal abortion care starting in the 1920s. Another aunt couldn't afford to continue her accidental pregnancy because she already had two children and a new job. My mother had medical complications and ended a pregnancy two years after my birth. These were abortions that occurred in the 1930s, 1960s, 1970s, and 1980s. I was told about fear, risk, logistics; sadness and gratitude; husbands, bad boyfriends, kids; money, sex, and zero guilt.

But all that stuff, the texture of everyday existence, is not what we talk about regularly. While women have been publicly acknowledging their abortions for years—from *Ms. Magazine*'s famous open letter in 1972 to viral Twitter campaigns mounted on hashtags like #ShoutYourAbortion— the swift affirmation of having had an abortion is different from detailed storytelling about it. The reproductive rights movement has "not figured out our relationship to abortion storytelling," says Debasri Ghosh, head of the National Network of Abortion Funds. "We have not figured out how to use it in service of the future that we hope to build, even pre-*Dobbs.* There's been a lot of stigma around the right kind of abortion stories, the wrong kind of abortion stories."

This isn't just some soft, sad problem of experiences unshared. It's been a serious tactical error. The comparative absence of mainstream storytelling about what abortion was like under *Roe*—not only about the many kinds of abortions that took place but also about the ones that were impeded by the Hyde Amendment and restrictive laws at the state level—left millions unaware how incomplete *Roe* had been, and how effective the encroaching anti-abortion forces on the right had become at eroding it.

My friend Zoe has just started speaking publicly about a third-trimester abortion she had four years ago in part because prior to her own experience, she'd had no knowledge of the roadblocks that existed under *Roe,* even in blue states. "As someone who always used to call myself pro-choice, and who now calls myself pro-abortion, I had somehow never heard the story of someone who needed a later abortion," she says.

After the detection of a severe problem with the fetus, she was told by her doctors that she would have to fly to another state to get the abortion she needed. "I was absolutely shocked when I found out that I was past the legal limit in New York, which I had always thought was this liberal oasis where you could get any care you needed," she tells me.

After her procedure, she found support and community thanks to a thirty-two-week abortion story told to Jia Tolentino, then a writer at *Jezebel,* by Erika Christensen, who is now a full-time later-abortion patient advocate. Now Zoe is telling her story. But she is also aware of the pitfalls, since her experience—as a middle-class married white woman whose abortion was in response to a fetal anomaly—could be leveraged as one of the "good" kinds of later abortions, thus stigmatizing others, when what she wants is the reverse. "Abortion shouldn't be accessible just because you have a sad story," she says. "Nobody should be forced to stay pregnant for any reason."

Without people who have had abortions describing their realities, the empty space has been filled by punitive, *anti-*abortion storytelling—at the center of which is the imagined character of the fetus and its "personhood." Michele Goodwin, law professor and author of *Policing the Womb: Invisible Women and the Criminalization of Motherhood,* recalls sitting through a hearing at which an anti-abortion lawmaker held up a piece of fabric the size of a salt packet and announced that it was a diaper for a baby "born alive after abortion," which is not a real thing.

"It was absurd," says Goodwin, who pointed out that the space ceded to these false narratives has led to "claims that there are such things as heartbeats" at six weeks gestation, "which there aren't," making their way to the Supreme Court. Meanwhile the stories of providers who have had to retrofit clinics, do unnecessary transvaginal ultrasounds, and recite misinformation to satisfy state restrictions have gone unheard.

Countering false narratives is partly what led Goodwin to write in *The New York Times* of the abortion that ended her pregnancy, at age twelve, which was the result of being raped by her father. Goodwin says she took her tale to the press "because we have so devolved in government that I thought this needed to be told, because there's no public understanding at all. There is not a human face." She was all too aware of the assumptions made about victims of sexual abuse and incest: that their lives are messy and therefore less sympathetic or believable. "Mine is a life a lot of people would look at and say, 'She's a law professor and lives a pretty decent, healthy life, but this could happen to her.' And yeah, it happens to people like me too."

Describing an abortion is a fraught ask for many reasons. "The idea that if women don't tell their stories of abortion, they might lose access to it is really troubling," says Goodwin. "It reminds me of 'Sing for your supper' or 'Dance if you want to stay alive tonight' on slave plantations." Then there is the fear absorbed from generations of illegality; before *Roe,* getting an abortion was contingent on silence. After *Roe,* too, when clinics were bombed and providers murdered, and abortion seekers regularly had to run a gauntlet of protesters, keeping quiet could be a protective measure. And it's difficult to overstate the degree to which the shame and stigma heaped on abortion seekers over generations—via media, religious messaging, pop culture, and politicians—has been internalized by many women.

Despite being raised in a pro-choice family, Renee Bracey Sherman didn't tell anyone when she had an abortion in 2005. At the time, she had no narrative context for how she was feeling. She was isolated in part because the abortion stories she did know about had come primarily from white women in whom she couldn't see her own biracial identity reflected.

"The reason I didn't talk about it was because I didn't see anyone around me saying, 'I had an abortion,'" says Bracey Sherman, who went on to found We Testify, a group dedicated to telling a wide range of abortion stories, centering the experiences of people of color and others on the margins of mainstream narratives. "Every time I saw abortion argued about on television, it was always some Catholic bishop. None of them were talking about race. They were talking about nothing that was relevant to nineteen-year-old me."

As a young activist, Bracey Sherman was regularly told by mainstream pro-choice organizations that storytelling didn't work as a communicative tool or, worse, that it was harmful to the movement, she says. The movement surely wanted to get the word out that lots and lots of people have abortions, but specifics could easily spin out of their rhetorical control. For many of the biggest reproductive organizations, abortion stories served as carefully calibrated transactional vehicles used to extract a vote from a politician or a donation from a rich person.

In this context, those who wanted to control the stories could be a little like Goldilocks: the narratives couldn't be too happy lest they be perceived as cavalier; they couldn't be too sad lest they give the impression that abortions are tragedies; the abortions couldn't have been too late, or too casual, or too tied to sex or ambition or pleasure or self-interest. "We're still fighting about which stories get to get told," says Bracey Sherman. "If it's, 'My abortion was great, I took the pills at home, it was wonderful,' that's considered frivolous. There's always some regulation: It's never the right time; it's never the right type of story."

The fewer stories that get told, the more representational weight each one carries. Each individual narrative is asked to stand in for so much, rather than exist simply as one grain of sand on a beach's worth of reproductive experience. In the lived world, abortion isn't some heavily weighted reality siloed off from the rest of life, health care, and humanity. Abortion *is* life, health care, and humanity.

"Imagine if there were an archive and the understanding that that archive would lead to," says Goodwin. The failure to build that archive was political malpractice. Because while some pundits and Democrats can barely suppress their gleeful fantasies about an army of women angry about *Dobbs* storming the polls in November and saving their electoral skins, there has been no accounting for the fact that many people don't yet fully understand that this loss is a human rights crisis. The accumulation of that knowledge, and the fury that will come with it, is going to take longer to build than the Democratic consultant class realizes.

In recent years, when the tenuousness of *Roe* had finally begun to penetrate, even some politicians, including Representatives Pramila Jayapal, Barbara Lee, and Cori Bush and Senator Gary Peters, have told their own abortion stories. In coming weeks and months, we are likely to be awash in more abortion stories as the shock of the new world seeps in. Many will frame this era as a return to an old world; the coat hangers will get dragged out in an effort to argue that we have moved backward. Which, legally, is true enough.

The idea that we have moved *only* in reverse, however, is its own distortion. Thanks to medical advances, especially medication abortion, the future will not look the same and will involve fewer coat hangers and many more safe and effective pills. No thanks to the expansion of our carceral state, the perils ahead will be different from those of our past. Republicans and Democrats have spent the last five decades making the criminal justice system ever more monstrous, particularly for Black, brown, immigrant, and poor populations; it now stands ready to absorb new categories of criminals.

The additional horror is that the value of abortion stories may be about to shift in a sickening direction. We are at a terrible crossroads at which the stories of abortion—the testimony—may go from being a tool that could have been deployed on behalf of those needing care to a tool used against them.

"How do we protect storytellers?" asks Bracey Sherman. Speaking of some who have worked with We Testify, she says, "we have a number of storytellers who self-manage their abortions. I want them to be able to share their stories, and I don't want to have to visit them in jail. And in a lot of places, your story is a confession. And that is what I'm super terrified about in this moment."

This piece is published by permission of the author and Vox Media, LLC. It was originally published on June 30, 2022, at www.thecut.com/article/rebecca-traister-post-roe-v-wade-untold-abortion-stories.html.

———

REBECCA TRAISTER is a writer-at-large for *New York* magazine and *The Cut* and the author of *Good and Mad*, about the history and political power of women's anger.

GET REAL

JENNIFER BAUMGARDNER

I was two years old when *Roe* was handed down, so I don't remember that day-and-night shift in women's stature. I do remember being attached to the pro-choice issue at a young age, though. Partly sincere and partly to get attention, I was the sole student to claim to be pro-choice in some pre-election tally of hot-button issues at my grade school in Fargo. My mother's feminist friend gave me a coat hanger button with one of those red *Ghostbusters* circle–backslash symbols over it to pin on my ski jacket, which I wore with pride. My immediate family was, as we always put it, openly "pro-choice," an identification that felt bold in our conservative state.

And yet, looking back, the abortion part of pro-choice was an abstraction. By this I mean that we didn't know anyone who had had an abortion, nor did we know anyone who had placed a child for adoption. Unwanted pregnancy happened to other people. It took me years to understand that of course we knew many people who'd had both experiences, but that we, unconsciously and out of ignorance rather than bad intent, had colluded in keeping real people's real experiences out of our dinnertime conversation and thus out of the official history. You could chalk this up to midwestern repression, except it happens everywhere.

The summer before my sophomore year in high school, I intersected for the first time with the realities of having a reproductive system. A charismatic recent South High grad impregnated my sixteen-year-old sister, a National Merit Scholar readying herself for senior year. In 1985, pregnancy was reason to rescind these scholarships—just one of the reasons my sister wanted an abortion. She didn't tell the guy or my parents, and instead turned to me and a friend on the basketball team who'd had an abortion the year before.

We quickly discovered two of the many hoops she'd need to clear: a $260 fee (far more money than any of us had access to) and a bypass of North Dakota's parental notification law, which my sister needed to go before a judge to secure. The timeline for procuring cash and court approval was tight. She was already a little more than three months out from her last period. There has always been just one clinic in North Dakota, and a doctor flies in from out of state once a week for procedures. If she missed that week's window, she'd be too far along for the vacuum aspiration procedure they provided.

Desperation bred creativity: I borrowed the money from a senior I hardly knew and rode my Schwinn to the clinic, where my sister was waiting for the last-minute cash handoff. A woman who worked at the clinic accompanied my sister to a judge's private chambers, where she was asked a few questions about why she wanted to have her records sealed. Her reasoning was, in effect, I'm a good kid and I want my parents to continue to think I'm a good kid.

"I didn't have the emotional maturity to do anything but what I did," she told me recently. Immediately after the abortion, bleeding and cramping, my sister rode her bike to varsity basketball practice, so as not to seem suspicious. As for the guy, she never involved him at all; "I felt like it was my problem."

This was a very fucked-up enterprise that, fortunately, turned out alright. Even in a conservative state, my sister had the autonomy and support to be able to get the abortion she wanted and go on with her life. She eventually told my parents, and they were stunned that she'd go to these lengths, including asking me (of all people) to help her, rather than coming to them for support and money and help with what was, no doubt about it, a crisis. After all, we were a pro-choice family.

Unvarnished stories of unplanned pregnancies are tamped down in our culture—and by culture, I mean all of us—our collective id, our hive mind. Years into a journalism career in which I wrote frequently about abortion, I'd never quoted anyone on the record about their actual experiences—but I was drowning in political rhetoric. So in 2000, when I was nearing thirty, I began working with some of the WLM activists who'd theorized the idea that "women were the real experts on abortion" and created the speak-outs that played a crucial role in repealing New York state's abortion laws in 1970. With a group that included Ellen Willis, Alix Kates Shulman, Barbara Seaman, Florence Rice, Ros Baxandall, and many other luminaries of the second wave, we produced a speak-out event called "No Restrictions" at Judson Church. Judson was itself an historic site—it housed the Clergy Consultation Service on Abortion, wherein a group of rabbis and pastors referred women to physicians willing to provide safe abortion service pre-*Roe*. This was the concrete, straight-from-the-woman expertise I needed to aid my own understanding of how abortion rights relate directly to human rights.

In 2003, I wrote an article in *The Nation* asking people to contact me with their own abortion stories for what I began thinking of as the I Had an Abortion Project. I wanted to put real faces and stories on the "issue," to make it clear that women who had abortions weren't evil people you didn't know but human beings you knew and loved, like my sister. I was inundated with handwritten letters and emotional emails filled with riveting, years-repressed reality. I asked my friend Gillian, a documentary filmmaker who had just had a baby, to help me film thirty or so of the people who'd reached out. Together, we gathered in-depth interviews from Loretta Ross, Byllye Avery, Gloria Steinem, Dawn Lundy Martin, Amy Richards, and many others about abortions legal and illegal. The stories—heartbreaking, terrifying, hilarious, brave— broke some spell for me, and I don't think I ever used the word "pro-choice," or really any of the other jargon surrounding this subject, to describe experiences of pregnancy again. The documentary we made is called *Speak Out: I Had an Abortion* (Women Make Movies) and there is a companion book as well, *Abortion & Life* (Akashic), with portraits and stories.

The key for me back then, and perhaps even now that *Roe* has been overturned, is bridging the gap between what we say we believe and our lives. We say that we believe that women have the right to decide when and whether to give life, but we treat the reality of our abortion experiences as too hot to handle, TMI, not suitable for polite conversation. Abortion experiences are treated like pornography or public displays of same-sex affection in the 1980s, when there was grudging tolerance that queer people couldn't help it, but did they need to flaunt it!?

Testing this idea, in 2004, an election year, I made and distributed brown T-shirts with the words "I had an abortion" printed in blue. A simple statement of reality for so many, yet it was by far the most controversial thing I've ever done. It launched a thousand op-eds and letters to the editor, full of outrage, from people who identified as pro-life and pro-choice. To me, the response to the shirts, and the fear and exhilaration people reported they felt wearing them, revealed how uncomfortable we still were with abortion, even as we had the right to it. The first time I wore one of those T-shirts in public, I felt a bolt of trepidation—a scared, illogical sense of being in the wrong that didn't match up with my conscious thoughts, like when I dropped my Bible at church right before my first communion and this thought surged: *Wait, will I be punished for this?*

I've had two kids and one abortion at approximately nine weeks. That was in 2010, when my second child was just under one. Apropos of something, I mentioned I'd had an abortion when my oldest, Skuli, was about eight. He remarked, "Because you're my mother, I think I should be pro-abortion, but as a kid, I think I should be pro-life."

We sat with the logic of his formulation for a while. His understanding of abortion was that it prevents a kid from coming into existence, and I wanted to validate that this is true. It made sense to him to want more kids in the world, regardless of context. "The first bad emotion kids feel is powerlessness and not being allowed to do things," Skuli told me when we recently revisited this memory. "The idea of more kids in the world, generally, reverses that dynamic."

I didn't explain that day that women died when they didn't have access to abortion or that far more pregnancies end in spontaneous abortion (i.e., miscarriage) than induced abortion. I did say that the vast majority of people who seek an abortion are already mothers. They are choosing not to create a new life in order to have enough money, energy, and time to take care of the children they have.

A few years later, I was talking to both kids about a work issue, and how I was feeling nervous because I was going to have to fire an employee. "I think you'll be good at it," my younger child, then five or six, said. "I mean, you fired our sister." I nodded. "That's one way of putting it."

When I share this story, people sometimes rush to reassure me that I didn't "fire" a "baby," but I welcomed that window into their understanding of me and feminism—and life, too. The policing of language around sex and reproduction particularly irks me. "Correcting" someone who calls a fetus a baby, for instance, or insisting on the term anti-choice for "pro-life," obfuscates how defensive and ashamed most people feel about sex and women's reproductive power. Besides, I was more intrigued that my children had decided this pregnancy would have yielded a sister, had it progressed. So, we talked about why they were picturing a sister, and then we talked about how we all start off with the same genital structures in the womb until differentiation, which occurs six or seven weeks into a pregnancy.

My kids are seventeen and twelve now, and lately we've been talking more about the realities of adoptees and birth mothers because I've been coproducing staged readings of Katie Cappiello's latest play, set in a maternity home in Worcester, Massachusetts, in 1963. In my lifelong attempt to understand and shore up abortion rights, I came late to trying to understand this pregnancy outcome because it seemed to me, I'm ashamed to say, less of a feminist issue. Then, in 2006, I read Ann Fessler's *The Girls Who Went Away: The Hidden History of Women Who Surrendered Children for Adoption in the Decades Before Roe v. Wade.*

Reader, that book changed me.

First, it is deeply researched and beautifully written. Second, it is a feminist act to create space for these suppressed stories. What I learned from *The Girls Who Went Away* is that what is now casually on offer as a fix for the overturn of *Roe* has a truly shameful, silenced history. During the pre-*Roe* years, when sex education was almost nonexistent and birth control difficult to obtain, girls who "got pregnant" were often sent to maternity homes. Upon giving birth, they surrendered their babies, under duress, to "nice families." More than 1.5 million infants were placed for adoption between 1945 and 1973 in closed agreements. These women, mothers all, were fed a constant drip of enforced gratitude. They were so lucky, given their wretched sins, for having a place to go, for the couple that deserved to be parents who would take the baby, for the chance to go back home again as if this had never happened—as if growing another life, laboring and delivering alone, and having one's baby taken away had never happened. Poof. If you care about women at all—or even if you hate women, but care about babies—you owe it to your soul to digest these histories.

As we gird our loins for the fallout of this latest misogyny, I pray we will stay in touch with actual reality. The I Had an Abortion Project showed me how easily stigma is deployed to flatten profound experiences into mere rhetoric, divorced from the real people affected and the nuanced challenges of real life. To me, owning your abortion and adoptions experiences, if you've had them, demonstrates that you believe they are not shameful but rather the very essence of political conversation.

Here is a reality check: A pregnant person has the power to give life and, ipso facto, the power to not give life. There is no shame in that.

OUR BODY IS OUR OWN

RUBY SALES

I was raped by a neighbor and became pregnant at fifteen. My first reactions were shame, fear, and self-recrimination for getting myself into this mess. The thought of my mother's hurt and disappointment hung over me like a menacing cloud, threatening to bury my fifteen-year-old Black girl self in a morass of depression and hopeless despair. Every day and almost every hour, I ran to the bathroom hoping to discover that my period had finally come, and that the baby I feared was growing in me was nothing more than a bad dream.

On the fifth week that my period did not come, I at last threw myself into my mother's arms and wailed out the truth. I expected her to lash out at me with fury and condemnation. Instead, she held me and demanded to know what had happened, as well as the name of the father. At the mention of his name, and upon learning that he raped me while posing as a good friend of the family, my mother exploded with a torrent of damnations and curses against him, both for raping me and for his betrayal of my parents' trust.

Soon enough, however, that righteous anger turned into a kind of helpless rage on my mother's part—because she understood that the law allowed men to rape women and girls without any legal constraints or punishment. There was nothing to be done to him; I alone would suffer the consequences. In this moment, my mother and I were united, not only by our grief but also by our identities as Black women in the South—our intersecting realities of race and gender rendering us the least protected, and the most sexually violable, by any man, white or Black.

I was raped and impregnated in the 1960s, when the legacy of enslavement continued to prop up practices that reduced Black women and girls, legally and socially, to sexual objects and commodities for the taking of all men, especially white southern ones. Individual- and state-sanctioned terror, sexual crimes, and the general dehumanization of Black women were all legitimized to satisfy the demands of a post-enslavement industrial complex, predatory masculinity, and a lust for absolute power and mastery over all of our lives and bodies.

Within this circle of shared pain and common history, I found in my mother the comfort and courage to release the heavy burden that weighed like lead upon me. And although my mother and I tunneled through the initial stages of my revelation hand in hand, we both understood that we had yet another hill to climb: what to do about the pregnancy.

I knew that my mother was passionately and deeply against abortion because every day, in her profession as a nurse, she saw with her own eyes "how little the medical profession valued the lives of pregnant Black women and girls, as well as their unborn fetuses." As a frontline worker on the OB/GYN ward in the local hospital, my mother was a witness to the heinous and dehumanizing history of illegal sterilization, experimentation, and other medical crimes committed by white doctors against Black women. These doctors saw Black motherhood, childbearing, and fertility as grave threats to the sanctity of white life, culture, and power.

Southern Black women's passionate and nonnegotiable commitment to their reproductive right to birth children created in my mother and her peers feelings of great moral ambiguity about abortion: On the one hand, they did believe in the practice, in moderation. On the other, they struggled with the question—because it was nearly impossible to detach the procedure from the attempts of white men to control and contain Black life. As my mother put it to her friends, "Honey, some of these white doctors and hospital staff treat Black women who have babies like they have done something wrong. But it's a different story for white women, who everyone cheers for having babies."

Every day of her professional life, my mother looked these issues in the face—and she was absolutely determined to leave them out of her private life. As we grew up, my mother reminded my sister and me over and over again that if we became pregnant, she would not put blood on her hands by helping us get an abortion.

Now, here we were, with me pregnant and my mother forced to wrestle with the dilemma. Despite her love for me and her desire for me to have the best in life, my mother's decision to participate in my having an abortion was not easy. But after what seemed like a lifetime of thought, to my shock, my mother turned to me and declared, "You must have an abortion." Over the years, I would come to understand the vast and complex moral territory my mother had to navigate in order to meet me in the moment of my need.

Once my mother had made the decision, she reached out to my teacher for help. Both of these women who mothered, loved, and protected me joined hands in finding a person to perform an illegal abortion. They identified a Black nurse who performed the abortion in her bedroom by inserting a hard, cold tube into my uterus. The following day I awoke with an alarmingly high fever from a life-threatening pelvic infection. Thanks to a white doctor with whom my mother worked, I survived—unlike several girls in my community who died at the hands of abortionists. As was the case for many Black girls in the South, they died as a direct result of the criminalization of abortionists (mainly women) and abortions, which forced these practitioners to work underground in unsanitary, unsafe, and often lethal environments.

Ultimately, someone turned the nurse who'd given me the abortion into the hands of white men, leaving it to them to adjudicate her guilt or innocence. This class of men—whose hands were stained with the blood of pregnant Black women, girls, and their fetuses, so many of whom they had lynched, shot, and burned alive—sentenced her to twenty years of hard labor in the Georgia penitentiary. She died there. Despite the official story, which reduced the expanse of this nurse's biography to a one-dimensional tale of criminality, the truth is, in fact, more complex. Even though members of the white southern establishment saw this woman as a menace to society, Black women and girls felt differently. She was, for us, a way out of a dead-end road, offering possibility in culture where white leaders refused to imagine any future for us that didn't involve being a concubine, wife, or mammy.

Within this culture, my mother's decision to help me secure an abortion was a radical act of resistance that stretched her beyond rigid lines to actively imagine a more expansive future. Understood thusly, my mother's actions carried the handprints of generations of southern African American women who imagined a future for their daughters and other Black girls, and stretched themselves profoundly to bring it into being. These women, like my mother, acted on a staunch unwillingness to cede to southern white men the power to control and own the bodies of Black women and girls. They created for each other a life-affirming womanishness where Black women and girls, rather than white men, were powerfully significant in each other's lives. Their feats of resistance would become the walking stick for generations of Black women who would forge for themselves and their daughters lives grounded in the soil of pragmatic optimism, despite the white supremacy and misogyny they faced.

On Friday, June 24, 2022, with their 6–3 decision to overthrow *Roe v. Wade*, the Supreme Court's right-wing, extremist justices put a scalpel to the right of women to have dominion and power over our bodies and lives. Their decision lays another brick on the foundation of white supremacist and misogynistic movements, which for the last fifty years have sawed away at the territory gained in the freedom struggles that began in the 1950s and stretched to the 1990s—gains that radically unsettled and unraveled the absolute power of white supremacy and misogyny in America.

The decision to overturn *Roe v. Wade* represents a full-throated pushback on the assumption, fought for and won by women's movements, that our lives and our bodies belong to us. The loss of *Roe* is a universal blow for all women—and yet, given the significance of color in this nation's history, the decision strikes a particular blow at Black women, who, in a culture where power and control are always constructed around gender, race, sexuality, class, and religion, will be disproportionately impacted by the machinations of this court.

If, as our foremothers did, we now desire a different version of life for women and girls, we must stretch ourselves to bring that reality into being. To that end, it is imperative that our movements of the 21st century operate from intersectional freedom discourses—ways of thinking and being that knit together the universal and the particular. We must understand that we are joined by more than what separates us; fragmenting and erasing our relatedness only serves the forces of white supremacy and misogyny that have dogged our culture for so long. Because the guardians of systemic power construct hierarchical structures of domination around our differences, we tend to respond by building movements in which we either eradicate those differences or turn away from them. In doing so, we end up replicating the same problematic approaches we are contesting. We certainly see this in some pro-abortion conversations, which often center the lives of white women—as if all the women are white and all women live the same lives.

Now, in order to address the issues that led to the reversal of *Roe v. Wade*, we in the movement must relinquish our attachments to us/them discourses—whether they demand self-righteous conformity or create monolithic narratives that stymie dissent or erase our particularities as women. We can no longer afford to banish each other to the non-redemptive ground of "enemy."

Rather, our movements must have room for women like my own mother—women who, with legitimate concerns, still wrestle with their own ambiguity concerning abortion. We must treat these women not as enemies but as potential sojourners for gender power. History teaches us that self-righteous judgment is a pathway to vigilante, rather than restorative, justice; it is a repetition of the destructive strategies of the status quo. The right wing, it is worth noting, took a different approach to building their movement. They recognized and used some women's ambiguity on the issue to slowly grind away at *Roe v. Wade*.

In the short and long run, women's movements for gender power must systematically break with the culture of oppression and divisiveness that has defined us for so long. Leaving the old ways behind, we must now build redemptive movements—ones in which we see each other whole, thereby weaving together the many threads of our identities.

RUBY SALES is a social critic and long-distance runner for justice. She believes that a universal starting point for justice is the question, *Where does it hurt?*

FACING HIGHER TEEN PREGNANCY AND MATERNAL MORTALITY RATES, BLACK WOMEN WILL LARGELY BEAR THE BRUNT OF ABORTION LIMITS

CECILIA LENZEN

The Texas Tribune

Linda Goler Blount, president and CEO of the Black Women's Health Imperative, says she grew up with the ability to make choices about her body because her mother's generation fought for the right to abortion care.

She laments the same won't be true for the Black children who will mature into womanhood without that access and worries about the effects that looming abortion restrictions across the country will have on them.

"The state is telling them that they're not valuable, that they can't be trusted to make the best health care decisions for themselves, that they're not worthy of being able to make these choices," Blount said.

The US Supreme Court ruled in June to overturn *Roe v. Wade*, eliminating the constitutional protection for abortion and allowing states to set their own laws regarding the medical procedure. In 2021, Texas passed a "trigger law" that would go into effect if *Roe* were repealed and make it illegal for patients to get an abortion with few exceptions. The trigger law is set to go into effect in August of 2022.

Lawmakers and reproductive rights advocates like Blount say Texas's abortion ban will disproportionately affect women of color, particularly Black women, who already face higher risks of health complications or death related to pregnancy or childbirth. Taking away the right to abortion care will likely lead to an even higher risk of health complications and mortality, higher teen pregnancy rates, and increased financial burdens.

State Rep. Jasmine Crockett, D-Dallas, said the justices and lawmakers who supported the Supreme Court's ruling have the privilege of wealth and class that will make it unlikely they'll ever have to feel the effect of these laws—but Black women will.

BLACK WOMEN FACE GREATER HEALTH RISKS

In addition to Texas, twenty-five other states are certain or likely to ban abortion now that *Roe v. Wade* has been overturned, according to the Guttmacher Institute. Blount said it won't be long in the coming weeks and months before the US begins to see the long-term effects of those bans on Black women.

Black women in the US are more likely to die from pregnancy or childbirth than women in any other race group, according to a 2018 report from the National Partnership for Women and Families. Black women are three to four times more likely to experience a pregnancy-related death than white women, and the risk spans income and education levels.

Black women are also more likely than other racial groups to experience maternal health complications throughout the course of their pregnancies. And hospitals that predominantly serve Black communities provide lower-quality maternal care, performing worse than others on twelve out of fifteen birth outcomes, including elective deliveries, nonelective cesarean births, and maternal mortality, according to the report. About 75 percent of Black women give birth at hospitals that predominantly serve Black patients.

There's a variety of reasons why these statistics are higher for Black women, Blount said. Black women often lack access to proper prenatal care. If you're Black with low income and living in rural areas, you just don't have the access, she said.

In addition, Black women in the US are more likely than their white counterparts to be obese, which can increase the risk of gestational diabetes, hypertension, preeclampsia, and other pregnancy complications, Blount said. Weight gained and kept after giving birth, along with limited leisure-time physical activity, may especially contribute to obesity among Black women, according to a study by the National Heart, Lung, and Blood Institute. Black women also appear to be particularly susceptible to cultural, psychosocial, and environmental factors that can promote weight gain.

Because of high chronic stress and race-based trauma and fear, the majority of Black women produce about 15 percent more cortisol, a stress hormone, than white women, which in turn raises the risk of pregnancy complications, according to the National Heart, Lung, and Blood Institute.

"And so literally, the combination of poor health, lack of income, lack of access, and the stress of being Black in this country causes premature mortality," Blount said.

And when Black women are ready to deliver, they are often devalued and dismissed in medical rooms during and after the delivery, Blount said.

Blount mentioned the experience tennis star Serena Williams had shortly after the birth of her daughter, Alexis Olympia. Williams said in a 2018 interview with *Vogue* that she had extreme shortness of breath after her daughter's cesarean birth and was concerned because of her history of pulmonary embolisms, a condition in which one or more arteries in the lungs become blocked by a blood clot. She told a nurse that she needed a CT scan and IV heparin right away, but her requests were dismissed because the nurse thought her medications were making her confused.

As access to abortion becomes more limited across the country, Blount said she anticipates Black maternal mortality rates to increase by 30 percent or more and Black poverty rates to increase by up to 20 percent. As mortality rates increase, so will rates of morbidity, or suffering caused by a disease or medical condition, she said. Many Black women will be left permanently disabled or sick long enough that they will lose their jobs, which will make caring for their families much more difficult. Black women are often the sole breadwinners in their household, but they also help take care of broader family and community networks. When a Black woman becomes sick or unable to work, it causes a ripple effect through their community, Blount said.

All these factors contribute to Black women being the largest demographic of abortion-seekers in the US, Blount said. Black women account for 38.4 percent of abortion patients, the largest share among other racial and ethnic groups, according to 2019 data from the Centers for Disease Control and Prevention. That year, white women had the lowest abortion rate (6.6 abortions per 1,000 women), and Black women had the highest (23.8 abortions per 1,000 women).

In Texas, 18 out of every 1,000 Black women of childbearing age received abortions in 2019. Black Texans have consistently had the highest rates of abortion in the last decade compared with other groups, with rates five to six times those of white Texans and double those of Hispanic Texans. Black Texans make up about 12 percent of the population.

For Crockett, a Democrat lawmaker from Dallas who in 2021 voted against the state's law barring abortions after about six weeks into pregnancy, bans on the procedure are personal. As a Black woman of childbearing age herself, she worries about the scary reality of not having safe, legal abortion access.

However, Crockett said if she were to have an unplanned pregnancy, she could afford to travel out of the state to seek an abortion if she needed. The same won't be true for so many socioeconomically disadvantaged people of color in her district, she said.

She expects to see Black teen pregnancy and Black mortality rates skyrocket as women seek out illegal abortion access. If there are women willing to risk their lives for cosmetic surgeries like Brazilian butt lifts, Crockett said, other women will certainly be willing to take the risk of getting an illegal abortion for more significant issues like unwanted pregnancies.

BLACK MATERNAL MENTAL HEALTH AND FINANCIAL BURDEN

Kay Matthews, founder of Shades of Blue Project, said the abortion ban will also negatively impact Black maternal mental health. Her organization focuses on mitigating the mental health issues Black women face, and she has already seen an increase in demand since Senate Bill 8, which banned abortion after about six weeks of pregnancy.

"We are seeing the impact in a huge, huge way," Matthews, forty-three, said. "We're seeing this blanket effect of what's already been happening."

Almost 40 percent of Black people who give birth experience maternal mental health conditions, according to a 2021 report from the Maternal Mental Health Leadership Alliance. Compared to white women, Black women are twice as likely to experience maternal mental health conditions but half as likely to receive treatment for them. Such conditions include depression, anxiety disorders, obsessive compulsive disorder, post-traumatic stress disorder, bipolar illness, substance use disorders, and postpartum psychosis in rare cases, according to the report.

Matthews said she doesn't think lawmakers have considered the long-term effects of forcing people to keep pregnancies that they don't want. It's "mentally debilitating" to have to keep a child that you felt you weren't ready or prepared for, she said.

These days, life is expensive even for a single adult, Matthews said. Adding another person to take care of makes it so much more expensive, especially when the US is facing a diaper and baby formula shortage. She said many people think it's easy to combat those shortages, particularly the formula shortage, by simply breastfeeding. But that doesn't account for women who aren't able to produce breast milk or who have past trauma associated with their breasts, which is frequent among Black women.

"It seems like everything is falling apart and just our basic rights to make our own decisions about our bodies are now being taken away from us," Matthews said. "It's hard, and folks are struggling."

Even those who aren't pregnant and may not become pregnant soon are still being mentally taxed. Just the thought of "what if it does happen" is causing panic for many women, especially Black women, Matthews said. That can cause both a physical and mental toll.

For Black women, Blount said the underlying messaging of the Supreme Court's opinion and the looming abortion bans across half of the country is that their bodies aren't valuable and that they can't make decisions about their health care by themselves. This alone, she said, will undoubtedly cause long-term trauma among young Black girls as they become adults.

"I'm really concerned about this repeated trauma from this incessant messaging that young girls in Texas and other southern states are going to get over and over and over again," Blount said. "So in 15 [or] 20 years when they're adults and out in the workforce, what is this going to mean for them and their emotional well-being?"

As it is for Black women, stress and panic are facts of life, Matthews said. Black women have learned to push through and persist against countless barriers. This is another thing they will have to overcome. For now, the only thing they can do is collectively band together and share resources for support, she said.

WHAT ADVOCATES AND POLITICIANS CAN DO

Abortion experts and advocates say Texas and other states outright banning abortion should increase education and resources relating to pregnancy and childbirth to prepare people for the reality of forced childbirth. But some have very little hope the state will do so.

Instead, Matthews said she believes help will come from community leaders and organizers who work to share information and resources with the Black community.

Blount said organizations like hers will need to come together to fund abortion funds and find resources to help Black women. Her organization is currently working on plans to make abortion medication and Plan B readily and safely available to Black women in the South.

She said state lawmakers should make birth control and Plan B widely and easily available. Plus, they should expand Medicaid and provide better prenatal health care for Black women, and medical providers should listen to and trust feedback from Black women when following up on any health complications.

"There are steps that can be taken to reduce maternal mortality rates, but they start with valuing the very lives of these people who are giving birth," Blount said.

But one of the biggest things that not just Black women need to be focused on is voting, Blount said. The next election cycle will be highly focused on reproductive justice, and people who want to reinstate bodily autonomy must show up to the polls.

Crockett said she personally wants to ensure that pro-abortion organizations trying to assist abortion-seekers have the funds they need to do so. Plus, she hopes to see other Texas Democrat lawmakers expand resources for Black women.

"It is incumbent upon every elected official who gives a damn to at least make sure that they start going and meeting women where they are and making sure that if there are resources available, that we are educating them on what their options are and what those resources look like," Crockett said.

Historically, that hasn't happened, she said, and she has "no faith" that anything will be done on the state level to assist abortion-seekers.

"What can Texas do? A lot," Crockett said. "What will Texas do? Nothing."

This article originally appeared in The Texas Tribune, *a nonpartisan, nonprofit media organization that informs Texans—and engages with them—about public policy, politics, government, and statewide issues. It has been updated to reflect the passage of time.*

CECILIA LENZEN is a graduate of the University of Texas at Arlington and a 2022 summer reporting fellow at *The Texas Tribune.* She has worked as a fellow at the *Fort Worth Report* and freelanced for *The Dallas Morning News, Dallas Observer, Daily Dot,* and other Texas news publications. Previously, she served as editor-in-chief of *The Shorthorn,* UT-Arlington's student newspaper.

"ROE WAS THE FLOOR"

A Q&A WITH ELIZABETH ESTRADA, NATIONAL LATINA INSTITUTE FOR REPRODUCTIVE JUSTICE

Elizabeth Estrada has spent more than a decade working to build movements for reproductive health, rights, and justice at the state and national levels. She currently serves as the New York Field and Advocacy Manager for the National Latina Institute for Reproductive Justice, which fights for equal access to reproductive health for Latine communities. In the days leading up to the final SCOTUS decision on Roe, I spoke with Elizabeth about the coming threat to abortion access, the issues that matter most to the Latine community, and what gives her hope, even in these troubling times. The interview has been edited for clarity and length.

—EH

ELIZABETH HINES: Let's start by talking about you. What led you to the National Latina Institute? What motivates your work every day?

ELIZABETH ESTRADA: I am a Mexican immigrant who migrated to the United States in 1986, when I was four years old. What motivates me to do this work is *necessity*. I always joke that if it weren't for oppression, then I probably would be a choreographer or ballet dancer, my aspiring childhood dreams. But because oppression does exist, and access to abortion is not easy for folks with low incomes or immigrants or women of color like myself, I know I have to do this work.

It was really my first abortion, at age twenty-one, that activated me to fight for abortion access, given all the barriers I experienced accessing care. Barriers like lack of information; the deep stigma and silencing around abortion; misinformation that attempts to lead us away from accessing care; transportation to a clinic that was so far away from where I lived; and then, of course, money, having to pay out of pocket because my insurance didn't cover abortion.

All these challenges to access, and the procedure itself took fifteen minutes. This is a private health care decision that I made in consultation with myself, my loved ones, my family—and yet it was so difficult to access that care. It was that experience that really brought me into my activism and why I do this work now. I just want to be a soft place to land for folks who decide to terminate their pregnancies, so that we can avoid the stigma and the shame I felt when I had my first abortion.

EH: Tell me about the Latina Institute and the reproductive health work you all have been doing, particularly right now.

EE: We're a progressive organization, and we work with activists across New York City and nationwide. We have a presence in New York, and in Virginia, Texas, and Florida. We work with community members to organize and mobilize around reproductive justice issues. But it's not only about reproductive health and rights—because, for an immigrant, a right on paper doesn't necessarily translate to real access to that right, whether we're talking about access to abortion, maternal care, or sex ed. This is an intersectional fight that we're addressing here, given the myriad barriers people face. For us, justice and dignity is such an important piece of the puzzle.

At the Latina Institute, we serve as a liaison between the community and a health care provider. So we'll work with partners at local independent clinics to get folks appointments, or on policy initiatives within each state and city. But our main goal is to empower Latines, provide them tools, and share education and knowledge with them so that they can become the leaders in their own communities. Reproductive justice aims to center the people most impacted by reproductive oppression, and we believe that the people most impacted are experts in their own lives. So we just share and provide tools and spaces for folks in the community to talk about these issues, learn about reproductive injustices, and then advocate for themselves.

EH: How do people in the community find out about your organization?

EE: A lot of people get to us by word of mouth. I would say that the majority of folks that I organize with here in New York have come to me and said, "Hey, my friend Elaine talked to me about Latina Institute, and I just want to know what you-all do."

What we hear from folks is that we provide a safe space to talk about feminist shit. Often, our own families are not really comfortable talking about sexual and reproductive justice, so our spaces allow for intergenerational groups of feminist people to join the circle and not only build consciousness but also have a safe place to talk about queer liberation, abortion, maternal mortality, homophobia—and then we equip them to talk about those issues in their own community.

We often say, the courts aren't going to create access for us. So it really can start with a dinner-table conversation that opens up and perhaps helps to destigmatize abortion and sexual health.

EH: As we speak today, the Supreme Court is on the verge of overturning *Roe v. Wade*. Assuming Justice Alito's leaked draft is where we're headed, how will the Latina Institute respond?

EE: Well, like many of our partners, we plan to be out in the streets. And while that is not our only tactic, it's really important for folks at home to see us out there, so that 1) we relay a clear message to our community members that they're not alone in thinking that this is unjust, and 2) we show the court that we're not going to go out without a fight.

But this reality is not new for us. At the Latina Institute, much of our work has already centered on creating access and providing information for our community, because so many have not had easy access to abortion services for quite some time. For example, in the Rio Grande Valley in Texas, which sits on the Mexico and Southern Texas border: this is a largely immigrant community that has lived without real access to abortion for many years already, and certainly not since SB 8 was introduced in September of 2021. I would say that many folks in the Bronx also face significant barriers to access, given limited transportation. And while New York covers abortion under a Medicaid program, there's still a really big issue here with religious stigma, in addition to trying to avoid fake "clinics," aka crisis pregnancy centers (or CPCs).

We know that after the decision, we'll likely see a huge influx of folks to New York coming from Texas, from Florida, from Oklahoma, and other abortion restrictive states. We've already seen this increase since the passing of SB 8 in Texas. We collaborate with partners at the New York Abortion Access Fund (NYAAF) who have told us that their caseload has increased 100 percent since September of 2021. So, we will be strengthening our partnerships locally here in New York and across the state with abortion and other practical support funds, ramping up our collaboration with local independent clinics, and campaigning to inform our community about how to avoid fake "clinics," because they only terrorize abortion seekers and cause more harmful delays in access to vital care.

We also want to create spaces where folks can come if they want to cry, or if they just need to rest. For women of color and Black and Indigenous communities, while this decision is detrimental to our lives, many of us have already been living without true "choice" for a long time. So, it's important to hold our communities close and let them know that it's okay to rest.

This fight is a marathon, not a sprint—and that's not just a tag line. We must rest in order to keep fighting for the long term.

EH: Not every community wrestles with the same issues around abortion. Are there particular challenges that the Latine community faces on this issue that you think most people aren't aware of?

EE: I was born in Mexico, raised in Atlanta, and I now live and work in the Bronx. These communities are largely Black and brown, and a lot of our cultural issues when it comes to abortion are similar. There's a lot of stigma. We have a faith-based community. But for the Latines that I have talked to here in New York and across the United States, the ability to access health care—abortion, yes, but all the other things, too—is a huge issue for us. Our staff often speak to Latine women who don't receive much preventative care. They go to the doctor or the hospital only when they have to, when they're so sick that they have no choice. They forego preventative care because they don't have access—or perhaps because they fear they might run into NYPD, or a checkpoint, like they have in the Rio Grande Valley, Texas, and get stopped by immigration officials.

The issue of immigration enforcement is one that has a huge impact on our community. Passing progressive immigration reform has been a priority for immigrant communities for many, many years, and not just for Latine communities: the largest community of immigrants being deported and mistreated are actually African and Black Caribbean immigrants. So we see the fight for TPS (temporary protected status) and comprehensive immigration reform as critical for the Latine community.

When we poll folks in our community, we see that 80 percent of Latine voters believe women should have the ability to choose whether to terminate a pregnancy, without any interference of a politician. So, if you put it plainly like that—"Should you be able to decide for yourself, about your own body?"—it's very easy for our community to say yes, absolutely. No politician should be involved in private health care decisions. But access to sexual and reproductive health care continues to be a top priority for the Latine community, as well as immigration reform, incarceration, and surveillance by the police.

EH: What worries you most about life in the post-*Roe* era?

EE: It makes me really emotional to think about. I have the privilege of volunteering for the New York Abortion Access Fund. Oftentimes, when people call the Spanish hotline, I talk to folks who think that they have absolutely no options, and that they might be forced to carry a pregnancy to term. Today, I can reassure them that we'll be able to help. We'll pay whatever you need, whatever it takes, and we'll connect with other abortion funds in other states to help crowdsource funding for any client that calls in needing funds for abortion care. What scares me is the possibility that I'll soon have to tell pregnant people that they won't be able to get the funds they need for their abortions.

Disinformation and misinformation worry me, too. Oftentimes, you see federal policies being covered on the Spanish-language news and they only add to the misinformation. As a result, you'll see folks here in New York saying, "Oh, wow, I didn't even think that I could have an abortion. I thought it was illegal everywhere." That kind of misinformation leads to delays, leads to life-altering decisions, and I worry that people will end up confused and intimidated in all states, even the ones that don't have restricted access. I am also concerned that fake "clinics" will more forcefully attempt to step in to replace legitimate health care providers in this new reality, because we've already seeing legislation that uses CPCs interchangeably with real providers.

Many of us reproductive justice workers come from countries like Mexico, Honduras, the Dominican Republic, Colombia, that are now advancing and decriminalizing abortion. In El Salvador, women have been jailed for miscarriages. Folks in the US don't think that can happen here, but it has, and that's my biggest fear of all: that people will miscarry, be accused of self-managing an abortion, and then be met with prosecution and incarceration. Communities that have high Latine and Black populations already face the threat of a police state. With abortion bans, prosecution and incarceration will only increase.

EH: There's so much to worry about in this landscape—is there anything in your work that makes you feel hopeful?

EE: One positive development is that there has been a huge emphasis on centering the voices of BIPOC who have had abortions and listening to our leadership and understanding how best to fight against reproductive oppression. That has really heartened me because it reminds us that storytelling continues to be a powerful source of transformation, of culture shifting, of compassion and moving people into the reproductive justice movement.

I also find hope in all the support we're seeing for abortion rights across the country. The people of the United States overwhelmingly support individuals' decision-making autonomy and reproductive freedom. They're on the side of abortion. Whether they believe they would have one or not, the vast majority supports the right to self-determine if and when to start a family—and that is extremely important, because it means our movement is growing and strengthening.

As the reproductive justice movement expands, I'm motivated by the centering of Black leadership in this fight. Black reproductive justice organizations like SisterSong belong at the helm of what a future without *Roe* may look like. I love seeing white allies come to this movement and heed the leadership and listen to the voices of the Black women who created the reproductive justice movement. I'm here to welcome folks with open arms, to listen, to educate, and to be agitating out in the streets. *Roe* was the floor, and I am certain we can imagine a far more just and equitable solution to enshrine access to abortion for anyone who needs it, for whatever reason.

***

ELIZABETH ESTRADA is the NY Field and Advocacy Manager at the National Latina Institute for Reproductive Justice, where she engages in movement-building, develops community leadership, builds relationships with key stakeholders,

HOW THE SUPREME COURT DECISION LIMITING ACCESS TO ABORTION WILL HARM THE ECONOMY AND WOMEN'S FINANCIAL WELL-BEING

MICHELE ESTRIN GILMAN

The Supreme Court has overturned *Roe v. Wade*, the landmark case that gave women the right to terminate a pregnancy. This is devastating not only to the bodily autonomy and dignity of women, but also to the economy.

Access to reproductive health lets women control the timing and size of their families so they have children when they are financially secure and emotionally ready and can finish their education and advance in the workplace. After all, having children is expensive, typically costing almost US $15,000 a year per child for a middle-class family. For low-income working families, childcare costs alone can eat up over a third of earnings.

Reproductive health is about more than the right to abortion. It's also about access to family planning services, contraception, sex education, and much else—all of which have also come under threat in recent years.

Providing Americans with a full range of reproductive health options is good for the economy, as well as essential to the financial security of women and their families. As a law professor who represents people experiencing poverty, I believe doing the opposite threatens not only the physical health of women but their economic well-being too.

THE ECONOMICS OF CONTRACEPTION

A Supreme Court majority acknowledged as much in 1992, stating in its *Planned Parenthood of Southeastern Pennsylvania v. Casey* decision:

> *The ability of women to participate equally in the economic and social life of the nation has been facilitated by their ability to control their reproductive lives.*

But in recent years, the right to control their reproductive health has become increasingly illusory for many women, particularly the poor.

Given their focus on limiting access to abortion, you might assume that conservative politicians would be for policies that help women avoid unintended pregnancies. But conservative attacks on birth control are escalating, even though 99 percent of sexually active women of reproductive age have used some form of it such as an intrauterine device, patch or pill at least once.

In addition to its widely recognized health and autonomy benefits for women, contraception directly boosts the economy. In fact, research shows access to the pill is responsible for a third of women's wage gains since the 1960s.

And this benefit extends to their kids. Children born to mothers with access to family planning benefit from a 20 percent to 30 percent increase in their own incomes over their lifetimes, as well as a boost in college completion rates.

Not surprisingly, in a 2016 survey, 80 percent of women said birth control had a positive effect on their lives, including 63 percent reporting that it reduces stress and 56 percent saying it helps them to keep working.

DISPARITIES IN ACCESS

Still, there is a class divide in contraception access, as evidenced by disparities in the 2011 rate of unintended pregnancies—the latest data available.

While the overall rate fell to 45 percent that year from 51 percent in 2008, the figure for women living at or below the poverty line, although also decreasing, was five times that of women at the highest income level.

One reason for this disparity is the cost of birth control, particularly for the most effective, long-lasting forms. For instance, it typically costs women over $1,000 for an IUD and the procedure to insert it, amounting to about one month's full-time pay for a minimum-wage worker lacking insurance coverage.

These costs are significant, given that the average American woman will have about two children and will thus need contraception for at least three decades of her life.

Unfortunately, publicly funded family planning meets only 54 percent of the need, and these funding streams are under constant attack by conservatives.

Not surprisingly, health insurance makes a difference, and women with coverage are much more likely to use contraceptive care. And yet about 6.2 million women who need contraception lack insurance coverage.

Further, this coverage can be denied to millions of employees and their dependents who work for employers claiming a religious or moral objection under a Supreme Court ruling in 2020.

SEX EDUCATION AND THE ECONOMIC LADDER

Another key to reproductive health—and one that isn't discussed enough—is sexual education for teenagers.

For years, the public has spent up to $110 million a year on abstinence-only programs, which not only fail to reduce teen birth rates but also reinforce gender stereotypes and are rife with misinformation. Low-income minority teens are particularly subject to these programs.

Teens without knowledge about their sexual health are more likely to get pregnant and less likely to work, spiraling them to the bottom of the economic ladder.

ACCESS TO ABORTION

Then there's the issue of abortion. Even in states that retain a right to abortion under the new legal regime, the cost can be prohibitive for some women.

Half of women who obtain an abortion pay more than one-third of their monthly income for the procedure.

The longer a woman must wait—either because state law requires it or she needs to save up the money, or both—costs rise significantly. Studies show that women who cannot access abortion are three times as likely to fall into poverty as women who have obtained abortions.

HYDE AND HEALTH

Another way in which US policy on abortions exacerbates economic inequality, especially for women of color, is through the ban on federal funding.

It has been so since the 1976 enactment of the Hyde Amendment, which prevents federal Medicaid funds from being used for abortions except in cases of rape or incest, or when the life of the mother is at risk.

Denying poor women coverage for abortion under Medicaid contributes to the unintended birth rates that are seven times as high for poor women as for high-income women.

The overturning of *Roe v. Wade* will impact the poor the most. Women who are denied abortions are more likely to end up in poverty, be unemployed, and turn to public assistance.

By contrast, economists have established that the legalization of abortion led to improved educational, employment, and earnings outcomes for women, as well as for their children.

Politicians cannot promise to grow the economy and simultaneously limit access to abortion, birth control, and sexual education. America's economic health and women's reproductive health are linked.

This article was originally published by The Conversation *(theconversation .com). It has been updated to reflect the Supreme Court decision to overturn* Roe v. Wade.

MICHELE ESTRIN GILMAN is the Venable Professor of Law and the Associate Dean for Faculty Research and Development at the University of Baltimore Law School. She is also a director of the Center on Applied Feminism, which works to apply the insights of feminist legal theory to legal practice and policy.

TO IMAGINE A WORLD
WITHOUT *ROE*,
LOOK TO KENTUCKY

APRIL SIMPSON AND MELISSA HELLMANN

The Center for Public Integrity

For eight days in April of 2022, Kentucky was the only state in the nation without access to abortion services. A sweeping law that banned abortions after fifteen weeks also included new requirements for providers, which the state's two clinics said they couldn't meet.

Reproductive health organizations worked to overcome new barriers to abortion in one of the nation's poorest states. Hotline operators at nonprofit Kentucky Health Justice Network scheduled out-of-state services for clients, arranged child care, and secured hotel rooms for overnight stays. Volunteers drove people without access to transportation 113 miles north to appointments in neighboring Indiana. The state's abortion funds helped shoulder the cost of services for those who couldn't afford them. Kentucky's EMW Women's Surgical Center and Planned Parenthood resumed abortion services after a federal judge temporarily blocked enforcement of the state law in late April.

The "roller coaster ride of emotions" foreshadowed what was to come in Kentucky, said the nonprofit's operating director, Ashley Jacobs. On June 24, the US Supreme Court overturned *Roe v. Wade*, pushing decisions to regulate or ban abortion to the states. Kentucky's anti-abortion advocates moved swiftly. As of August 2022, abortion is illegal in the rural state, except to prevent maternal death or permanent injury, with no exceptions for rape or incest.

In a post-*Roe* world, Kentucky is one of roughly half the states that have prohibited or are expected to roll back abortion services. People of color and low-income people will be disproportionately harmed by state restrictions and bans of abortion services, and are most likely to be criminalized for seeking care, researchers say.

According to the Pew Research Center, 59 percent of US adults say that abortion should be legal in all or most cases.

THE MOST IMPACTED

Childbirth can be difficult, even dangerous, for some women, said Candace Bond-Theriault as her eleven-month-old son whimpered in the background. Black women, in particular, face a high and rising maternal mortality rate. They die from pregnancy-related causes at three times the rate white women do.

"It's dangerous and no one should be forced to go through that experience if they don't want to," said Bond-Theriault, director of racial justice policy and strategy at the Center for Gender and Sexuality Law at Columbia Law School.

State restrictions may also force people to delay abortions, and safety risks increase the further along in a pregnancy, said Guttmacher Institute's Senior Research Scientist Liza Fuentes. Two-thirds of people accessing abortion care live in poverty, she added, which makes arrangements such as taking time off from work a heavy burden.

In jurisdictions that require parental permission prior to receiving abortion services, adolescents who can't safely disclose their pregnancies to caretakers could be in danger, she added. About 57 percent of pregnant people who obtain abortions are ages twenty to twenty-nine, followed by 31 percent in the thirty to thirty-nine age group and 9 percent up to the ages of nineteen, according to data from the Kaiser Family Foundation.

Restrictions that ban Medicaid coverage of abortions particularly affect Black and Latino people.

Since rates of unintended pregnancies are highest among low-income people and people of color, those populations will be most vulnerable to arrest and prosecution for violating state restrictions to obtain abortions, Fuentes added.

"When we think about what it means for abortion restrictions to harm people, we have to understand that it is taking place in the same healthcare system and criminal justice system that has perpetuated inequities that harm Black and brown people," Fuentes said.

In Kentucky, low-income and rural Kentuckians will be affected the most, said ACLU Kentucky spokesperson Samuel Crankshaw. The landlocked state is bordered by other states that have prohibited or are likely to ban abortion in the future, including West Virginia, Ohio, Indiana, Missouri, and Tennessee.

"People are always going to need abortions whether it's legal or not, and people with the most resources are always going to be able to leave and go somewhere where it is safe to do that," Crankshaw said.

In November, Kentucky voters will weigh in on the future of reproductive health care through a proposed state constitutional amendment: "To protect human life, nothing in this

Constitution shall be construed to secure or protect a right to abortion or require the funding of abortion."

"A lack of sexual and reproductive health care access has already had dire consequences for Kentuckians," Planned Parenthood of Kentucky spokesperson Nicole Erwin said in an email. Kentucky has one of the highest teen birth rates in the country.

A RELIGIOUS HISTORY OF ABORTION RESTRICTIONS

About 77 percent of white evangelical Protestants say abortion should be illegal in all or most cases, according to the Pew Research Center.

But when *Roe* was initially handed down in 1973, most evangelicals deemed it a "Catholic issue," said Randall Balmer, a historian and religion professor at Dartmouth College. Evangelicals weren't too concerned about it.

Some leaders spoke out—in favor. W. A. Criswell, then-pastor of First Baptist Dallas and a former president of the Southern Baptist Convention, issued a statement supporting reproductive choice. Two years prior to *Roe*, and twice afterwards, the Southern Baptist Convention publicly expressed its support for abortion rights.

But as the '70s drew to a close, conservative leaders like Paul Weyrich, considered the architect of the religious right, sought to galvanize a political movement in defense of exempting taxes from institutions like Bob Jones University and other religious schools with racially discriminatory policies, Balmer said.

First, Weyrich argued that these places should maintain their policies supporting racial segregation because they were exercising religious freedom. When that didn't work, he made his next move: Shift attention to abortion, Balmer said.

"I've described it as a godsend for the religious right because it allows them to divert attention from the real origins of the movement," said Balmer, author of *Bad Faith: Race and the Rise of the Religious Right*.

In Kentucky, where nearly 80 percent of the population are Christians, some in the religious left who support access to abortion services are speaking up. The Kentucky Religious Coalition for Reproductive Choice—an interfaith group that advocates for reproductive rights and provides education—distributed stickers to inform people about the availability of medical abortions and to spread the word that abortions were still legal following the leaked draft opinion of the US Supreme Court in May.

The coalition's national chapter grew out of the Clergy Consultation Service, formed in 1967, a group of faith leaders who referred people to trusted abortion providers prior to *Roe v. Wade*.

"You can be a person of faith and choose to have an abortion, and this is a decision that is not against God," said Carol Savkovich, vice chair of Kentucky Religious Coalition for Reproductive Choice.

Kentucky has been hit hard by abortion restrictions in recent years. The state had one abortion provider in 2017, down from seventeen in the 1970s. After the election of a Democratic governor in 2019, providers increased to two, both located in Louisville.

Civil rights organizations worry that other landmark Supreme Court decisions that rely on similar language, such as *Obergefell v. Hodges*, which ensured marriage equality, will also be at risk now that *Roe* is overturned. In the decision, Alito wrote that abortion is not a constitutional right, nor is it implicitly protected. Rights the Constitution does not mention should be "deeply rooted" in history.

The rights to have an abortion, to marry, and to have access to contraception are rooted in the rights to "liberty, privacy, and individual autonomy," Omar Gonzalez-Pagan, counsel and health care strategist at Lambda Legal, said in an email following the leaked draft opinion last May. He called the overturning of *Roe* an "assault" on the "many other rights that are premised on the liberty and autonomy protected by the Fourteenth Amendment, including the right to marriage equality."

A WAY FORWARD

Now that *Roe* is overturned, there may be opportunities to push for stronger state laws to improve health care access, said Aimee Castenell, southeast region communications director for the Working Families Party.

"As important as *Roe* is, in terms of actual access to health care, it has not been the most useful thing," Castenell said. "So I think moving outside of this idea of what *Roe* can and cannot do will create a space to have stronger laws that are beneficial to the people who need health care."

With the focus on states, this year's midterm elections carry even greater weight. Voters will elect candidates for 35 US Senate seats and all 435 US House seats. At the state level, 36 governorships and hundreds of state legislative positions are open.

"We will be able to take control of this narrative if we don't slip into some fascist nightmare," Castenell said. "But in order to do that, we have to be engaged."

This article was originally published by the Center for Public Integrity, a nonprofit investigative news organization based in Washington, DC. It has been updated to reflect the overturning of Roe v. Wade.

APRIL SIMPSON joined the Center for Public Integrity in October 2020 as a senior reporter covering racial equity. She was previously the rural issues reporter at Stateline, an initiative of The Pew Charitable Trusts. Before joining Pew, April was associate editor of *Current*, where she covered public media and won recognition for her #MeToo investigation of a veteran reporter.

MELISSA HELLMANN is an award-winning reporter who covers racial, gender, and economic inequality. Prior to joining the Center for Public Integrity in August 2021, she covered marginalized communities for *The Seattle Times*. She previously worked at *Seattle Weekly*, the Associated Press, *YES!* magazine, *TIME Asia*, and *SF Weekly*.

SOCIETY MAKES A CHOICE
BEFORE ANY OF US CAN

SORAYA CHEMALY

*"Women will always find a
way to have abortions."*

This past decade, as anti-abortion legislation has risen across the United States, it's a phrase I've heard over and over again: "Women will always find a way." This, alongside "It will never actually happen," has now been joined by other, similar statements as we confront the end of *Roe v. Wade*— "Underground networks are already springing up"; "There are pills now, you know." You might hear comments like these shared between friends in a coffee shop, or around a dinner table populated by people who aren't immersed in reproductive rights and justice movements. They rely on the idea that any woman can "choose" to have an abortion—and, now, she can choose whether or not to break the law and commit what may be a felony to do so.

It's true: People will find ways to end pregnancies—legal or not, safely or not. But what does it mean to foreground this idea of "choices" in our understanding of what it takes to access abortion? What do we miss when we suggest that choice plays any part in this narrative? Choice is almost always a matter of individual discretion, leading us, as a society, away from context, history, systems, and relationality. It is based on disconnection when what we vitally need is connection.

As a response to what happens now that *Roe* has been overturned, these assertions about choice (women will find a way; there are other options now) seem mainly meant to appease and distract, to deflect attention and fend off the possibility of further discomfort in conversation. The details of abortion, like those of menstruation, pregnancy, miscarriage, ectopic pregnancies, pre- and post-natal depression, infertility, and infant deaths, do make people uncomfortable, given how much shame and denial are attached to the issue. These offhand remarks about the future of women's access to reproductive health options are not of the type that tend to open doors to more discussion, more information, more knowledge, and greater understanding. Easier, instead, to reduce the complexity to a person's choices—and thus their individual, private responsibility for what happens to them.

For decades, the "abortion debate" has centered, and remains stubbornly centered, on this language of choice—the deficiencies of which, as a framework, have been well plumbed. As a generation of reproductive justice advocates has effectively argued, "choice" framing has meant calibrating our politics to the needs of the most privileged in our society (more affluent, primarily white women for whom abortion access is not a primary problem, economically or socially) and ignoring people who must confront the enduring legacies of slavery in our institutions, medical system, and economic lives. It has meant subsuming the dangerous realities of living in Black and brown bodies in America, particularly female bodies historically violently exploited for reproduction, in the pretense of equal choice for all. "Choice"—rooted in individualism—erases contexts, systemic inequality, and societal irresponsibility.

An abortion procedure may be a specific moment in time, but the human right to abortion is one that diffusely touches every aspect of a person's life and, in the aggregate, the fundamental rights of entire classes of people in a society. Choice distills abortion into moments: the moment of sex, the moment of decision, the moment of a procedure, the moment of possible regret. "Abortion"—the idea of it, the fact of it, the necessity of it—far exceeds moments. As we know, abortion is as relational, economic, and societal a concern as it is a personal one. "Choice," and even "abortion rights," simplistically flattens the diffuse and complex array of needs and impacts implicated in abortion. Pregnancy and birth, meanwhile, affect every aspect of a person's life: physical well-being, mental health, self-concept, personal and professional relationships, whether or not they might pursue education, and their ability to work for pay, secure housing, and establish financial stability.

In the end, however, no level of affluence or proximity to power can fully offset the risk of pregnancy in America, or the misogyny and misogynoir embedded in our societal ignorance of what it means to live in a body that can gestate life. Moreover, choice additionally plays into the hands of anti-abortion forces. When abortion is reduced to individuals and their choices, it becomes easier to categorize certain choices as "bad" and label the people who make them as irresponsible, misguided, or even evil. It is easier to claim they are in need of paternalistic oversight and rules to help them make "better decisions," in lieu of looking at the society or systems that produce undue risk and harms.

This isn't care—this is domination. A pro-choice, pro-abortion person has no interest in telling other people what to do with their bodies or forcing another person to have an abortion. With stunning consistency, however, the theoretically "pro-life" movement involves people and leaders who openly leave children living with food scarcity and mired in poverty; deny climate change and its disparate impacts on already marginalized communities; and refuse to regulate guns, even as men with guns sow daily tragedy across the nation. They are pro-control of women, their bodies, their reproduction, and their liberty—not pro-life—and their behaviors, too, are absolutely a matter of choice.

At its root, abortion is far more about how we care for one another as a society than it is about the choices we make as individuals. Caring for one another means making sure that people who can gestate are safe, get compassionate medical treatment when needed, and are able to work and live without fear, shame, and punishment. How we treat people who can have abortions is a referendum on how a society recognizes and values, or, quite pointedly, doesn't recognize and value certain lives, in particular the lives of those of us who can be pregnant and give birth.

At the most fundamental level, those of us capable of bearing children are repeatedly judged according to the normative experiences of those who cannot bear children at all. Even the standard for limiting abortion in the United States— fetal viability outside of a gestating body—is based on the reproductive experiences of people who cannot be pregnant. Historically, this has meant men, people who experience reproduction through separation. So a model of reproduction that is defined by the experiences of non-reproductive bodies (cisgender men), and based on separation, governs public and political understanding of reproduction and rights; meanwhile, we have virtually no standards, laws, rights frameworks, or epistemological bases that reflect the bodily knowledge of people who have been or can be pregnant. We don't even have the words to describe the experience of gestation—that of being both one person (the pregnant person) and another person (the fetus) simultaneously—accurately and clearly. Where would we find ourselves today if the experience of pregnancy—instead of ignorance about what it is like to live with a body that can be pregnant—informed our societal and political understanding of abortion?

It is no exaggeration to say that people who can reproduce are regulated like functional extensions of those who need us to reproduce, or that we are punished when we seek to address our own needs, exercise our freedoms, or access our purported rights. As individuals, we have no choice in these matters at all.

If abortion is indeed about any choice, it is about the choices a society, not individuals in that society, makes. So, "Women will always find a way to have abortions" actually means: "We choose not to care enough to ensure that people who need abortions can get them safely." It means, "We choose not to ensure that people who need abortions are safe, healthy, respected, and cared for" and "We choose not to care if some get sick, are impoverished, are traumatized, and die." It means, "We don't care if people who may need abortions live in a society that is hostile to their bodies, their safety and security, their equality and existence."

"Women will always find a way to have abortions" is another way of saying, "We choose to allow some people in our society to freely terrorize and oppress other people in our society."

A society that chooses to respect a person's decision to have an abortion, and that gives that person the ability to have that abortion without fear, danger, and stigma, is one that is committed to equality, happiness, freedom, health, and democracy. It is a society willing to challenge violent, patriarchal norms woven together with authoritarian, white supremacist ones.

Sadly, today, we are not that society.

To change people's minds, we need to change our language. To shape public understanding, we need to tell our stories loudly and make space for others to do the same. To challenge societal complacency, we need to shed shame about what it means and is like to live in a body that bears life. We have to use all the tools at our disposal to overthrow the past and those that cling with violence to it.

***

SORAYA CHEMALY is an award-winning journalist, author, and activist whose work focuses on inclusivity, feminism, violence, and free speech.

NO, JUSTICE ALITO, REPRODUCTIVE JUSTICE IS IN THE CONSTITUTION

MICHELE GOODWIN

Black women's sexual subordination and forced pregnancies were foundational to slavery. If cotton was euphemistically king, Black women's wealth-maximizing forced reproduction was queen.

Ending the forced sexual and reproductive servitude of Black girls and women was a critical part of the passage of the 13th and 14th Amendments. The overturning of *Roe v. Wade* reveals the Supreme Court's neglectful reading of the amendments that abolished slavery and guaranteed all people equal protection under the law. It means the erasure of Black women from the Constitution.

Mandated, forced, or compulsory pregnancy contravenes enumerated rights in the Constitution, namely the 13th Amendment's prohibition against involuntary servitude and protection of bodily autonomy, as well as the 14th Amendment's defense of privacy and freedom.

This Supreme Court demonstrates a selective and opportunistic interpretation of the Constitution and legal history, which ignores the intent of the 13th and 14th Amendments, especially as related to Black women's bodily autonomy, liberty, and privacy, which extended beyond freeing them from labor in cotton fields to shielding them from rape and forced reproduction. The horrors inflicted on Black women during slavery, especially sexual violations and forced pregnancies, have been all but wiped from cultural and legal memory. Ultimately, this failure disserves all women.

Overturning the right to abortion reveals the court's indefensible disregard for the lives of women, girls and people capable of pregnancy, given the possible side effects and consequences of pregnancy, including gestational diabetes, preeclampsia, hemorrhaging, gestational hypertension, ectopic pregnancy, and death. State-mandated pregnancy will exacerbate what are already alarming health and dignity harms, especially in states with horrific records of maternal mortality and morbidity.

To understand the gravity of what is at stake, one need only turn to the Supreme Court's own recent history. In 2016, Justice Stephen Breyer noted in *Whole Woman's Health v. Hellerstedt* that women are fourteen times more likely to die by carrying a pregnancy to term than by having an abortion. The United States bears the chilling distinction of being the most dangerous place in the industrialized world to give birth, ranking 55th overall in the world.

Disproportionately, those who will suffer most are poor women, especially Black and brown women. Black women are over three times as likely to die by carrying a pregnancy to term as white women. In Mississippi, a Black woman is 118 times as likely to die by carrying a pregnancy to term as by having an abortion. According to the Mississippi Maternal Mortality Report, from 2013 to 2016, Black women accounted for "nearly 80 percent of pregnancy-related cardiac deaths" in that state. At present, there is only one clinic in the entire state of Mississippi to serve hundreds of thousands of women that might need to terminate a pregnancy.

In 1942, in a unanimous decision delivered by Justice William Douglas in *Skinner v. Oklahoma*, the court explained that "This case touches a sensitive and important area of human rights," because Oklahoma sought to sterilize a man who committed petty crimes, including stealing chickens, under its "Habitual Criminal Sterilization Act."

Justice Douglas wrote that reproductive autonomy and privacy, associated with "marriage and procreation," are "fundamental," and a state's interference with such rights "may have subtle, far-reaching and devastating effects." The justices were concerned about the inequality at the heart of the law, which singled out poor and vulnerable classes of American men.

Now, eighty years later, Mississippi has already made a "clear, pointed, unmistakable discrimination," as if it has "selected a particular race or nationality for oppressive treatment," which the court specifically struck down and condemned in Skinner.

What today's Supreme Court strategically overlooks, legal history reminds us with stunning clarity, specifically the terrifying practices of American slavery, including the stalking, kidnapping, confinement, coercion, rape, and torture of Black women and girls. In a commentary reprinted in *The New York Times* on January 18, 1860, slavery was described as an enterprise that "treats" a Black person "as a chattel, breeds from him with as little regard for marriage ties as if he were an animal, is a moral outlaw."

Such observations were hardly unique or rare; the Library of Congress offers a comprehensive collection of newspapers, almanacs, daguerreotypes, illustrations, and other materials that comprise the "African-American Mosaic: Influence of

Prominent Abolitionists." Laws that date back to the 1600s expose the sexual depravity and inhumanity of American slavery. In 1662, the Virginia Grand Assembly enacted one of its first "slave laws" to settle this point, expressing, "Whereas some doubts have arisen whether children got by any Englishman upon a Negro woman should be slave or free, be it therefore enacted and declared by this present Grand Assembly, that all children born in this country shall be held bond or free only according to the condition of the mother."

Thomas Jefferson kept copious receipts and documents related to the births of enslaved children at his Monticello plantation, including those who were ultimately discovered to be his own. Not surprising, at the heart of abolishing slavery and involuntary servitude in the 13th Amendment was the forced sexual and reproductive servitude of Black girls and women. Senator Charles Sumner of Massachusetts, who led the effort to prohibit slavery and enact the 13th Amendment, was nearly beaten to death in the halls of Congress two days after giving a speech that included the condemning of the culture of sexual violence that dominated slavery.

Black women also spoke out about their reproductive bondage. In 1851, in her compelling speech known as "Ain't I a Woman," Sojourner Truth implored the crowd of men and women gathered at the Women's Rights Convention in Akron, Ohio, to understand the gravity and depravity of American slavery on Black women's reproductive autonomy and privacy. Reported by newspapers and recorded through history, Ms. Truth stated that she had born thirteen children and seen nearly each one ripped from her arms, with no appeal to law or courts. Wasn't she a woman, too? By the accounts of those gathered, including famed feminist abolitionist Frances Gage, the room stood still and then erupted in applause.

Similarly, in *Incidents In The Life of A Slave Girl*, published in 1861, Harriet Jacobs describes the Herculean efforts made to avoid the inevitable sexual assault and rape by her captor. She wrote, "I saw a man forty years my senior daily violating the most sacred commandments of nature. He told me I was his property; that I must be subject to his will in all things."

And yet slavery's vestiges persisted in Southern states, including within the domains of privacy, child rearing, and marriage. The Bureau of Refugees, Freedmen, and Abandoned Lands, better known as the "Freedmen's Bureau," founded March 1865, collected letters written by Black mothers despairing over vile "apprenticeships" whereby their children were kidnapped and returned to bondage under the guise of traineeships.

Congress followed in 1868 with the ratification of the 14th Amendment, which further secured the interests of Black women who had been subjected to cruelties inflicted on them physically, reproductively, and psychologically.

The 14th Amendment opens with the sentence, "All persons born or naturalized in the United States . . . are citizens of the United States and of the State wherein they reside," and as such would be protected by the laws of the United States. Such language applied to infants born to Black women, changing the provisions of law that had long denied Black children citizenship and the protection of laws. Lawmakers were understandably concerned about overturning states' laws that had denied children the dignity of personhood.

Justice Samuel Alito's claim that there is no enumeration and original meaning in the Constitution related to involuntary sexual subordination and reproduction misreads and misunderstands American slavery, the social conditions of that enterprise, and legal history. It misinterprets how slavery was abolished, ignores the deliberation and debates within Congress, and craftily renders Black women and their bondage invisible.

It is no hyperbole to say that the Supreme Court's decision in the *Dobbs* case is in league with some of the darkest rulings—*Plessy v. Ferguson*, which opened the floodgates to "separate but equal" laws that ushered in Jim Crow, and *Buck v. Bell*, which sanctioned states' eugenics laws permitting forced sterilization of poor women.

The court's central role—and, sadly, its complicity—in the harms that predictably will result from this decision cannot be overlooked. The court will be giving its imprimatur to states set to "trigger" laws that will criminally and civilly punish girls and women who want and need to end pregnancies, including victims of rape and incest, while ignoring the deadly traps in which most of those states have historically placed Black women.

"No, Justice Alito, Reproductive Justice Is in the Constitution," by Michele Goodwin, originally appeared in The New York Times *on June 26, 2022.*

MICHELE GOODWIN is a chancellor's professor of law at the University of California, Irvine, and the author of *Policing the Womb: Invisible Women and the Criminalization of Motherhood.*

REPRODUCTIVE JUSTICE ADVOCATES CAN'T AFFORD TO IGNORE HOW ABORTION BANS AFFECT ASIAN AMERICANS

JENN FANG

Prism

On June 24, 2022, the US Supreme Court struck down *Roe v. Wade*—a catastrophic decision that eliminated constitutional protections for abortion access and turned over control of reproductive rights to the states. The effects will undoubtedly hit hard for those who can become pregnant, especially among marginalized communities, and it's a struggle that Asian Americans of childbearing age in Texas have already been grappling with for almost a year.

Texas is home to the third-largest and fastest-growing Asian American population in the country, with an estimated nearly 250,000 Asian American women who are of child-bearing age residing in the state. In September 2021, Texas's abortion ban, known as State Bill 8, became by far the harshest in the nation and had already all but eliminated abortion access in Texas prior to the recent SCOTUS ruling. Clinics in Texas have been forced to turn away patients and stop offering abortion services, and many pregnant people are now crossing state lines seeking abortion care.

In contrast to model-minority stereotypes, 11 percent of Texas's Asian Americans are low income, and 15 percent lack health insurance or rely on Medicaid to cover their basic health needs. Low-income people of color are less likely to have access to early prenatal care and consequently are more likely to learn they are pregnant later than the ban's six-week mark. Low-income patients also typically rely on local free or low-cost clinics for their reproductive care, and most lack the resources to travel long distances to access an abortion.

Language barriers and immigration status present additional challenges to accessing reproductive care in Texas. Nearly half a million Asian Americans in Texas are English-language limited, and as many as one-fifth of undocumented immigrants in some Texas counties migrated from Asian countries. Immigrant women are also less likely to be able to travel farther than fifty miles to access abortion services, underscoring their reliance on local reproductive health clinics. It's not surprising, therefore, that 5 percent of patients nationwide who access reproductive health care through a Planned Parenthood clinic self-identify as Asian American.

Although detailed data of Asian American abortion rates in Texas aren't readily available, a series of studies in New York City—which is also home to a large Asian American population—found that roughly one-fifth of pregnant Asian Americans may seek an abortion, a rate comparable to that of non-Hispanic white women. Other studies suggest that this may be an underestimate: the Center for American Progress contends that as many as one-third of pregnancies in the Asian American community may end in abortion. Notably, the Asian American community is the only racial community in which abortion usage hasn't decreased in the last fifteen years, and abortion rates vary widely by patient ethnicity and immigration status. Among Indian women, for example, the abortion rate is as much as three times the average for the Asian American community at large. Similarly, abortion rates are on average 1.5 times higher for US-born Asian American women compared to foreign-born Asian Americans, even while the abortion rate has doubled among immigrant Asian women in New York City.

Some experts suggest the lower rates of health care coverage among Asian Americans, language barriers that limit health care access, cultural stigmas that hinder conversations on sexual health, and underutilization of early prenatal and contraceptive care can drive persistent gaps in sexual education among some segments of the Asian American population. This in turn contributes to higher rates of sexually transmitted diseases and unplanned pregnancy that drive these patients to seek out sexual and reproductive care, including abortion services.

DEMONIZED THEN RENDERED INVISIBLE

While attempts at passing near-total abortion bans like "fetal heartbeat" bills in eleven states have mostly been blocked by court order, Texas's SB 8 was the first to protect the state government from court injunction by empowering private citizens—not the state—with enforcement of the ban through vigilante harassment and lawsuits. In a climate already rife with anti-Asian hatred and racial intolerance, SB 8, now bolstered by the overturning of *Roe v. Wade*, exacerbates the threat of racial harassment and violence for Asian Americans and other people of color in need of abortion care in Texas.

Anti-abortion proponents have already used racist caricatures of Asian Americans as red herrings in their efforts to pass anti-abortion laws through state action, such as prohibitions against sex-selective abortion. These laws were ostensibly designed to prevent women from seeking an abortion based on the apparent sex of their fetus, a practice that the laws' supporters argue is commonplace in East and South Asia; in practice, they stigmatize abortions—particularly for Asian American women—and add additional layers of bureaucracy that further discourage women from receiving abortion care. Supporters of sex-selective abortion bans invoked anti-Asian xenophobia in arguing that state legislation is needed to protect America from the misogynistic influence of Asian immigrant women. This brutal and violent specter of Asian influence was so commonly used that one law review author explored how such abortion bans were also being advanced as an effort to discourage and curtail immigration by demonizing Asian immigrants.

Further, Asian American women have been among the first to be targeted by feticide laws originally designed to protect pregnant victims from domestic violence but which have recently been co-opted in some states to prosecute women who obtain an abortion or who miscarry their pregnancies. In Indiana, Chinese American Bei Bei Shuai was the first woman in the state's history to be charged with murder and attempted feticide after a failed suicide attempt in 2011 resulted in a miscarriage. Just a few years later, thirty-three-year-old Purvi Patel faced a twenty-year sentence for the termination of her pregnancy by what prosecutors argued was an abortion, even though she claimed she suffered a miscarriage; that sentence was eventually overturned by the Indiana Court of Appeals. These and other stories are clear evidence of the impact the anti-abortion movement has already had in criminalizing Asian Americans and their pregnancy outcomes. In an op-ed published in *The Washington Post*, former executive director of the National Asian Pacific Women's Forum (NAPAWF) Miriam Yeun described these laws as a coordinated effort to limit abortion rights by criminalizing Asian American immigrant women.

"Feticide laws, sex-selective abortion bans and similar legislation need to be seen for what they are—proverbial wolves in sheep's clothing," Yeun said.

DISREGARDED IN THE BROADER MOVEMENT

Unfortunately, Asian Americans have been otherwise rendered largely invisible in the discourse surrounding reproductive rights. In 1989, Dr. Laurie Nsiah-Jefferson concisely addressed the problem as one in which demographic data flattened the experiences of nonwhite women by presenting them under a single umbrella, "as if there were only two racial groups, white and nonwhite." Nearly thirty years later, studies still routinely fail to consider Asian American patients and their reliance on reproductive health services. The overall impact of restrictive abortion laws on the rights of Asian Americans is chronically disregarded, the distinct effect of these restrictions on individual Asian American ethnic groups is largely unknown, and Asian Americans are left out of the reproductive justice conversation, even among larger progressive movements.

While anti-abortion activists have unsurprisingly ignored the importance of abortion access for women of color, even supporters of abortion have historically excluded their voices, including those of Asian Americans. In the mid-1990s, a group of mostly white women were invited by the Clinton administration to consider proposed health care reforms that would include expanded reproductive health care access. The few Black feminists who were invited to attend were discouraged to find that this effort failed to consider the unique challenges that women of color face in accessing reproductive health care. Together they created the Women of African Descent for Reproductive Justice, which launched the modern reproductive justice movement. Soon after, the group expanded to become SisterSong, a multiracial coalition of reproductive justice groups that included Asian American feminists alongside Black, Latinx, and Native activists—all committed to applying an intersectional framework to the reproductive rights movement. Among these groups was the Asian Communities for Reproductive Justice—now known as Forward Together—which still centers the multifaceted impact of reproductive rights for Asian American women.

Despite this, mainstream advocacy for reproductive rights and health care continues to overlook both the impacts on—and the activism by—women of color. A study by the National Committee for Responsible Philanthropy recently reported that the top twenty recipients of reproductive rights funding are predominantly white organizations. For Asian American women, exclusion from the larger reproductive rights debate often comes in the form of deeply ingrained model-minority stereotypes that suggest that Asian American women are neither users of abortion services nor politically engaged in the reproductive justice movement; both misconceptions leave Asian American–led efforts under-resourced and invisible.

"It's been a fight to get [philanthropy] to fund us in a way that they fund some of the larger mainstream groups," former Forward Together executive director and activist Eveline Shen said in an interview.

CREATING THEIR OWN SEAT AT THE TABLE

According to Asian American advocates, the vast majority of Asian Americans support the legal right to abortion access. Their persistent exclusion from the fight for better reproductive rights and abortion access is a missed opportunity for the broader reproductive justice movement, but rather than waiting for acknowledgment from other activists, Asian American advocacy groups have wasted no time in advancing their own initiatives.

Asian American advocacy groups such as the NAPAWF—founded in 1996 to amplify the stories and issues of Asian American and Pacific Islander women and girls—continue to be vocal in pressing the issue of reproductive rights for and within the Asian American community. NAPAWF has challenged the racist rhetoric presented alongside sex-selective abortion bans in multiple states and in fighting the criminalization of pregnancy. In 2021, NAPAWF partnered with ten other Asian American advocacy organizations to issue a comprehensive reproductive justice agenda, presenting an intersectional framework for advancing reproductive justice alongside the need for systemic policy changes to address racial injustice, economic oppression, US militarism, and immigration reform, among other key issues. In Texas, NAPAWF was one of several Asian American reproductive justice groups to join the fight to overturn SB 8 and protect abortion access for Asian Americans and other marginalized people in the state.

"Asian American and Pacific Islander women are angry and tired of the long-standing efforts to restrict reproductive and abortion access," NAPAWF Executive Director Sung Yeon Choimorrow said in a statement. "NAPAWF will continue fighting until all AAPI women have complete access to the health care they need."

As part of this work, NAPAWF launched a new chapter in Texas to push for greater inclusion of Asian American voices in the fight for reproductive rights in the state. Asian American reproductive justice groups like NAPAWF and others are worried about the broader impact of anti-abortion laws on Asian American women's lives in Texas and across the country. Among their concerns are how anti-abortion laws based on xenophobic rhetoric will contribute to ongoing anti-Asian racism and violence, which NAPAWF has found already disproportionately targets Asian American women.

"For Asian Americans and Pacific Islanders, a reproductive justice framework acknowledges the diversity within our community and ensures that different aspects of our identity . . . are considered in tandem when addressing our social, economic and health needs," NAPAWF declared in their 2017 reproductive justice agenda. "The experiences and difficulties that an AAPI woman encounters are as diverse as the community itself."

Asian American women have been part of the reproductive justice movement since its inception. There is a long history in which Asian Americans have disproportionately suffered the consequences of anti-abortion efforts. Their work persists despite racist anti-Asian rhetoric by anti-abortion activists as well as the frustrating and ongoing sidelining of Asian American women's voices from mainstream reproductive rights organizing. While Black, Indigneous, and other WOC continue to work in concert with Asian Americans, the movement for reproductive justice won't succeed without actively embracing their efforts.

"All oppressions impact our reproductive lives," says SisterSong. "The intersectionality of reproductive justice is both an opportunity and a call to come together as one movement with the power to win freedom for all oppressed people."

This story was originally published by Prism on September 29, 2021, and was updated on August 4, 2022. Prism is an independent and nonprofit newsroom led by journalists of color. We report from the ground up and at the intersections of injustice: www.prismreports.org.

JENN FANG is a proud Asian American feminist, scientist, and nerd who currently blogs at Reappropriate.co, one of the web's oldest AAPI feminist and race activist blogs. Follow her on Twitter @Reappropriate.

ABORTION IS
A DISABILITY ISSUE

ROBYN POWELL

The fragility of reproductive rights in the United States has never been so clear. From the US Supreme Court's *Dobbs v. Jackson Women's Health Organization* decision, which overturned *Roe v. Wade* and nearly fifty years of legal precedent, to a rapidly growing number of states enacting laws limiting— and in some states, completely banning—access to safe and legal abortions, reproductive freedom is under attack at every turn. The *Dobbs* decision will have harmful consequences for all people, but most significantly for people with disabilities and other historically marginalized communities.

When disability is invoked in discourse concerning abortion, it is typically regarding abortions based on fetal disability diagnoses. Yet by framing disability and abortion only in the context of disability-selective abortions, activists, scholars, and policymakers fail to recognize that it is actual people with disabilities—not fetuses with disability diagnoses—who are harmed by abortion restrictions.

In a forthcoming *UCLA Law Review* article, I write about how disabled people have both an increased need for abortion services and decreased access. Simply put, people with disabilities must be included in all efforts to protect abortion rights.

The attack on abortion rights reflects the legacy and continuation of a history in which reproduction has been weaponized to subjugate disabled people and other historically marginalized communities. As such, disabled people are acutely aware of what happens when the government gains control of our bodies. In particular, people with disabilities have faced a lengthy history of threats to bodily autonomy, including forced sterilization. Eugenics aimed to "improve" the human race by restricting procreation of those deemed undesirable—disabled people, immigrants, Black people, Indigenous people, LGBTQ people, and incarcerated people. Black disabled people were especially subjected to forced sterilization.

Forced sterilization gained the blessing of the Supreme Court in the infamous 1927 *Buck v. Bell* decision. At seventeen years old, Carrie Buck, who was deemed "feeble-minded," became pregnant after being sexually assaulted by her foster parents' relative. To ostensibly hide the pregnancy that resulted from sexual violence, she was committed to the Virginia State Colony for Epileptics and Feeble-Minded, where her mother was also institutionalized. After giving birth, Buck's daughter, Vivian, was adopted by her foster family. The institution then sought to sterilize Buck per the state's involuntary sterilization law.

After a series of appeals, the Supreme Court upheld Virginia's law allowing institutions to condition a patient's release upon sterilization as constitutional. In reaching this holding, Justice Oliver Wendell Holmes Jr. stated that the forced sterilization would benefit Buck's welfare and that of society. He then proclaimed, "Three generations of imbeciles are enough." Following this decision, more than thirty states enacted compulsory sterilization laws. By the late 20th century, roughly 70,000 Americans, many of whom had disabilities, had been forcibly sterilized.

Even today, people with disabilities continue to endure state-sanctioned reproductive oppression. For example, a National Women's Law Center report published in January found that thirty states and the District of Columbia still have involuntary sterilization laws on their books. In these states, guardians, who are appointed by courts to make decisions on behalf of disabled people, are often the ones choosing whether a person is sterilized, even if it is against that person's wishes. Notably, research indicates sterilization is a standard procedure for disabled people. Guardians, also known as conservators in some states, are also permitted to make decisions about contraception, as demonstrated by Britney Spears's case.

Despite enduring a lengthy history of reproductive oppression, people with disabilities have been largely ignored in discourse about abortion rights. This exclusion is particularly problematic because overturning *Roe* will have devastating consequences for disabled people, who often use abortion services because they experience substantial disadvantages.

First, access to comprehensive reproductive health services, including abortion care, is crucial for disabled people because they are at greater risk of health disparities. According to research, people with disabilities have higher rates of maternal mortality and morbidity than people without disabilities. Moreover, some disabled people take medications that must be stopped prior to pregnancy. Without abortion services, disabled people who have unintended pregnancies will be put in an impossible situation: having to choose to suddenly end medication and risk harmful side effects, or continue medication that could harm them and their children.

Ultimately, restricting access to abortion will force pregnant people with disabilities to accept risks associated with pregnancy irrespective of their beliefs or health, placing some in considerable harm. This is both dangerous and cruel.

Second, abortion is important for people with disabilities because they experience severe economic disadvantages. According to the National Council on Disability, "people with disabilities live in poverty at more than twice the rate of people without disabilities." They also have considerably lower employment rates. These inequities are heightened for disabled people who are further marginalized. For example, Black people with disabilities are nearly 55 percent more likely than white people with disabilities to live in poverty. LGBTQ disabled people also experience substantial economic disadvantages.

In light of the dire economic circumstances experienced by people with disabilities, reducing access to abortion services will only worsen the situation. In fact, 49 percent of people who have abortions live below the poverty line, and many people seeking abortions do so because they cannot afford the costs associated with childrearing. Thus, it is reasonable to assume that some people with disabilities need abortion services because the disproportionate poverty they endure makes them unable to afford to raise children.

Even now, abortion is out of reach for many people with disabilities. Researchers estimate that the average cost of an abortion procedure at about ten weeks in the United States is just over $500, and the median cost of an abortion procedure at twenty weeks' gestation is $1,195. Given that most abortions are paid for out of pocket, these high costs can be prohibitive for disabled people. Moreover, a 2018 study found that twenty-seven US cities are "abortion deserts"—cities where people must travel at least 100 miles to reach an abortion provider. In addition to the high costs of abortions, which many disabled people cannot afford, some are unable to travel to an abortion provider because of lack of accessible transportation, especially in areas with limited to no abortion providers.

Ultimately, abortion access is essential for people with disabilities achieving some level of economic security. Some disabled people who have abortions likely do so because of their severe economic disadvantage, and increased abortion restrictions will only worsen these inequities. If abortion rights are further restricted, some disabled people will be forced to continue pregnancies and have children against their wishes and economic means, or they will seek unsafe methods of abortion.

Third, people with disabilities have inadequate access to reproductive health services and information, such as sex education and contraception, which makes abortion all the more important. Most people who have abortions do so because having a baby would disrupt their work, education, or ability to care for others. At the same time, research suggests that disabled people have higher rates of unintended pregnancies than nondisabled people. Disabled people also encounter significant barriers to accessing contraception, leading to decreased usage. Significantly, increased access to contraception is statistically associated with a reduction in abortion rates, which means that if disabled people had greater access to contraception they could be less likely to have an abortion.

The high rates of unintended pregnancies among people with disabilities likely also results from inadequate access to sex education and other information about reproduction and pregnancy prevention. Many students with disabilities are denied even basic sex education. And the increased rate of unintended pregnancies among disabled people is also likely a consequence of the inadequate reproductive health care available to them. In other words, the pervasive barriers that disabled people encounter when seeking reproductive health services and information—combined with the numerous inequities they experience—underscore the necessity of abortion rights for disabled people.

Finally, abortion access is significant for people with disabilities because they are uniquely vulnerable to sexual assault, intimate partner violence, and reproductive oppression.

People with intellectual disabilities are seven times more likely than others to experience sexual violence. Disabled people also contend with increased rates of intimate partner violence, which increases their need for abortions. People with disabilities are also at heightened risk of reproductive coercion. Thus, the high rates of sexual assault, intimate partner violence, and reproductive coercion experienced by disabled people likely contribute to increased rates of unintended pregnancies, and consequently an increased need for abortions.

In the aftermath of *Dobbs*, abortion rights activists must recognize the importance of abortion for people with disabilities. The bodily autonomy and self-determination that disabled people have fought so hard for will be completely undermined.

It will have devastating consequences for people with disabilities. It will bring us back to a time when the government controlled disabled people's bodies—something we are still fighting against today. Disabled people must be intentionally and fully included in all efforts to protect abortion rights. We can no longer wait.

This article was originally published by Rewire News Group (rewirenewsgroup. com). It has been updated to reflect the Supreme Court's ruling on Dobbs.

DR. ROBYN POWELL is an associate professor at the University of Oklahoma College of Law. Dr. Powell's scholarship focuses on reproductive justice, disability law, family law, and public health law.

COLLATERAL DAMAGE

ANN CRAIG

I never thought I would make the choice to have an abortion. In college, like many young women, I had a period that was so late, I thought I might be pregnant. Though the tests kept coming back negative, I had myself convinced that I was pregnant anyway. I was in no position to raise a child, but I was lucky enough to have a family that would support my decision to carry a child and give it up for adoption, if that is what I chose. So that is what I decided I would do while I waited for that positive test to show up: put the child up for adoption.

As fate would have it, I did not have to make any such choice that time around. The day I actually had to make the choice to end a pregnancy came much later in my life. I was thirty-six years old, married, and desperate to be a mother. I wanted that baby so much it hurt. I named her Jane, and I loved her. I still love her. Losing her was one of the most horrific experiences of my life, yet never once have I doubted that making the decision to terminate my pregnancy was the right decision for me and for my future family. Aborting Jane protected my life and the lives of my future children.

Trying to get pregnant over the age of thirty-five has its challenges. Advanced maternal age—the official diagnosis for pregnant individuals who will be thirty-five or older at delivery—is no joke. The chances of pregnancy decline, and the rates of health issues for both the fetus and the pregnant person increase. But I was healthy, in shape, married, happy. I knew the risks, but I was ready to bring a baby into the world. And I was lucky. My husband was on the faculty at a prestigious medical school. We had amazing health insurance, and it would cover virtually everything we might need.

After six months of trying, we were referred to a fertility specialist. At my age, he said, there was only a two-in-ten chance of a fertilized egg making it to a healthy delivery. So, this was going to be a battle—but I had faced uphill battles before. I was a Division I athlete in college who had not a shred of the talent needed to reach those athletic heights and yet had gotten there by never giving up, working every possible angle, studying my sport, and pouring countless hours into my training and preparation. Now that I knew the stakes, I knew I could do this. So, I relaxed into an old, familiar mindset. This was a game I could win.

The day I found out I was pregnant with Jane was wonderfully surreal. I was finally going to be a mom. Her dad and I were elated. All the stress of the trying evaporated, and we turned our attention to getting ready to become a family.

I knew the rules of the game, and I was ready. I followed every single recommendation by the American College of Obstetrics and Gynecology. I started drinking more milk. I stopped eating French cheese and deli meat and sushi. I stopped doing high-impact exercise and instead focused on walking and swimming. I made sure to get enough sleep and to see my doctor every four weeks, subjecting myself to the repeated weighing and prodding and poking.

Together with my husband, I evaluated the pros and cons of all the pre-natal testing available. We decided we would do the twelve-week nuchal translucency scan and blood test which would evaluate the baby's development and give a good indication of any major developmental issues. We decided we would not do the chorionic villus sampling (CVS) or the amniocentesis to test for genetic abnormalities because we did not want even the slightest risk to the pregnancy, nor did we believe that we would terminate a pregnancy with a genetic anomaly, such as Down syndrome.

The day I walked into the offices of the Prenatal Genetic Diagnosis Program began, as I remember it, as a glorious day. The sun was out, but the heat of the summer had not yet arrived. I could smell the nearby ocean as I approached the medical office's glass double doors. My husband was waiting for me there, an enormous smile on his face.

As we entered the building, I remember feeling absolutely giddy with excitement. This scan was going to be the first chance we had to see our baby. We sat in the waiting room and talked. Mostly we played the name game. Boys' names. Girls' names. Middle names. We wondered what our baby would be like. When I was called to the back, my stomach flipped. I breathed mindfully as I changed into my gown and climbed on the table; I wanted to remember every moment of that visit. The tiny fingers, the bent elbows, the growing baby who was nestled in my belly.

The technician smiled and exchanged pleasantries with us as she readied my little bump for the ultrasound. My husband and I squeezed each other's hands and looked at the monitor. We heard the familiar sounds of the heartbeat and then, suddenly, there was our baby. Moving, kicking, turning its head. Our baby was real. But the room was quiet. The technician had stopped chatting and was engrossed in her work, measuring and saving images. After some time, she excused herself and said the doctor would be in shortly.

When the doctor arrived, he repeated the scan. He measured each and every part of our little one, redoing the work the technician had just done. And that was when I realized something was wrong.

When the doctor finished, he turned to us with the same look my dad gave me when I was eleven years old and my cat died. My brain seized. I did not want to hear what came next.

Like anyone who has been through a terrible medical diagnosis can tell you, time almost stops when you first get news like this. Our child, the doctor said, was growing abnormally. The head was too big and the body too small. It was an early indicator that there was a significant, possibly severe disease or abnormality. He recommended we stay to have a CVS test that day. He would stay late to perform the procedure after his last patient.

I remember shaking my head—I didn't want a CVS test. I didn't want to risk the baby. Optimistically, I joked that maybe the baby just had a really big head. I come from a family of folks with big heads. His face filled with pity as he looked at me. "It's not a big head," I heard him say, "it's likely a genetic disease."

I don't think I cried. I am not even sure I felt anything at all. I agreed to the test, mostly because I wanted it to be wrong. I wanted him to be wrong. What could be wrong with that little wiggly, squiggly baby I saw on the screen? Surely that baby was perfect?

Several days later, I was at work when my phone rang. I had just very nearly managed to convince myself that the doctor was just being cautious, that my baby would be fine. I answered and it was my OB. She had the results of the test, she said; was there anywhere private I could take the call? I walked to my car and climbed in the driver's seat. My OB explained that my baby had been diagnosed with a condition called triploid syndrome, a condition caused by the presence of an extra copy of not just one chromosome but all twenty-three. Imagine having all of the various conditions, syndromes, and illness caused by all those extra chromosomes, all at once. I remember asking if this was caused by my age. No, she said, nothing to do with my age or my eggs. It was just a lightning strike, a rarity. The chances of a fetus with triploidy implanting and making it to second trimester were something like 1 in 10,000.

I remember asking if there was a way to know the sex of the baby. A girl, my doctor responded. In that moment, my baby became Jane.

The next several weeks were spent in Google black holes and in the offices of researchers and specialists. We met with geneticists, maternal-fetal health specialists, neonatal specialists. The response was consistent: Jane's condition was incompatible with life. She would be born, if she made it to term, with a Do Not Resuscitate order and a morphine drip. Neither her organs nor her tissue could be donated to living children due to the extra chromosomes, and no studies were being done on the disease. There was no possibility of treatment or of a cure. Jane was going to die, and, if she lived to see her birth day, she was going to die a horrible and painful death.

I thought that would be the worst of it, but I was wrong. During pregnancy, blood flows two ways across the placenta, and Jane's blood, with that entire string of extra chromosomes, was now floating around in my bloodstream. At the very least, this put me at a significant risk of preeclampsia, which could lead to seizures, organ damage, and heart disease. The worst-case scenario was that the additional chromosomes in my blood would lead to a choriocarcinoma, a type of uterine cancer that could end up requiring the removal of my uterus and end my ability to ever have a child of my own.

I was now left with an impossible decision to make, so I turned to my OB—a woman I had trusted with the most precious parts of my own body—and asked her if there was any advantage to waiting. No, she said very quietly, you are now at fifteen weeks. If you wait too much longer, termination will no longer be an option unless you are in immediate physical danger. You need to make a decision now.

So, I did. My husband and I met with a doctor willing to perform a second-term abortion. We had to visit his office after hours and be led through a back entrance. While pro-life activists hoping to save lives picket abortion providers and pray for souls, the trauma they inflict on patients like me, people already shattered by the horrors of their situation, cannot be underestimated.

The doctor presented us with our options. There were only two. The first was a dilation and evacuation. In this procedure, I would be fully anesthetized, the fetus would be removed, and my uterus cleaned out to prevent infections and preserve my chance for future pregnancies. The second was to induce labor and deliver Jane. I chose the latter, as I wanted the chance to be awake and present. I wanted to see Jane, to hold her. To tell her I was sorry. To show her she was loved and wanted. To make sure that she knew that she would forever be my firstborn child.

On the day of her delivery, I was led to the gynecology ward in the hospital rather than the delivery ward so that I would not have to hear the cries of healthy babies being born into the world. I had not eaten or had anything to drink since the night before. I was scared and hungry, and so tired. I found myself wondering if Jane would be able to take a breath so that she could be baptized, but I quickly pushed the thought out of my mind. Jane was going to die that day, a death I had chosen for her. I took another breath. Knowing this was the right thing to do didn't make it any easier.

After changing into a hospital gown and climbing to the bed, I was hooked up to monitors and an IV. I was given a morphine drip so that I would not feel any pain.

As soon as the nurse attached the drip, I knew something was wrong. My arm felt immediately hot. My heart rate sky-rocketed. I begged my husband to run for the nurse.

As it turned out, I was in the initial stages of anaphylaxis. The nurse swiftly detached the morphine drip and gave me an IV dose of antihistamine.

"How much morphine did I get?" I asked her.

"A single drop," she said.

The machine had not yet given a dose of the morphine. I had responded to the single drop on the end of the tube that had been hooked up to my IV.

In the process of delivering Jane, I learned that I have a lethal allergy to morphine—a fact that, eighteen months later, saved my and my son's life during his delivery. After more than fifty hours of labor with Matthew, the doctor wanted me to rest so that the baby, wherever he was stuck, might be persuaded to move and reposition himself. He asked the nurse to give me a dose of morphine. Because of what I had learned in delivering Jane, I was able to push back immediately. I could not have that drug. I was allergic, very allergic, to morphine.

Many hours later, holding my son against my skin and thanking God for his safe delivery, I asked the doctor what might have happened if I had been given that morphine at the dose he requested. The doctor sat quietly and picked up my hand. He looked me right in the eye as he said, "Either you or your son or both of you could have died." I knew in that instant that Jane had saved our lives. Her short time here was not meaningless, and her death was not senseless. Plain and simple. Jane was and is our guardian angel, a member of my family, a family that now includes three beautiful children, all of whom know about and love their sister, Baby Jane.

ANN CRAIG

I imagine what might have happened if I had not had the choice to end my pregnancy with Jane. If I were pregnant with her today, in the state of Texas where I reside now, I would not have had any option except to carry her to term or until she miscarried without medical intervention. My situation would fall squarely outside the bounds of a "health of the mother exception" in which my life was in immediate danger, even though carrying her significantly increased the risks to my health and my fertility. I wonder if I would have had the mental strength to weather such a pregnancy, knowing my baby was going to be born just to die. I wonder if my anxiety about my increasing age and my fertility would have had a lasting impact on my mental health. I wonder if I would have developed preeclampsia and had to deliver by C-section, possibly preventing me from any future vaginal delivery. I wonder if I might have developed a tumor in my uterus. Would I have had to decide whether to try to retrieve my eggs for a surrogacy or to adopt a child? I think about the financial burden that I would have had to carry during the pregnancy, the delivery, and the neonatal care Jane would have needed. My out-of-pocket expenses would likely have topped $10,000, not to mention the tens of thousands of dollars beyond that the insurance company would have had to pay the hospital and providers on our behalf.

I think about all of this, and then I look at my son Matthew and it all becomes clear. The tragedy for me, if I were pregnant with Jane now in Texas, is that he would likely not be here. This vibrant, smart, creative, silly, energetic, and snuggly nine-year-old boy would not, in all likelihood, be alive today. I ask myself how in the world these new laws and limits on abortion can be pro-life. From where I sit, abortion is health care—life affirming health care. Health care that allowed me to make a decision for myself that has resulted in my good health and the good health of my three children.

I am grateful that when I had to make this impossible decision, I lived in a state that provided me with accurate information and allowed me to make my own choice. My health care team, a team I chose for myself, stood by me throughout the process and in the days and weeks that followed. They treated me with kindness and respect, answering every question and providing me with every available option for treatment and care. Because of that attentive care, I am now the mom that I always longed to be.

In my case, this nation's new laws and regulations, including the reversal of *Roe v. Wade*, would not have supported life at all. Though they would have prolonged Jane's short life, the collateral damage might have been my life or the lives of my children, and I am not willing to accept a reality in which thousands of women become that kind of grist for the mill. I live in a state that prioritizes my right to bear arms above the right to make decisions about my own body. I live in a state that allows me to choose to go maskless or refuse a vaccine because no one can force someone to be physically uncomfortable for another person's benefit. Except, of course, if you are pregnant. Then all your rights to self-determination and bodily autonomy disappear, regardless of the consequences. I, for one, will not stand for this. Women can and must be trusted to make decisions about their own bodies for themselves. Just how a woman comes to make whatever choice she does is entirely her responsibility.

Losing Jane was one of the most difficult experiences of my life—but it was the right choice for me. Ensuring other women have the same ability to make those decisions is something I am willing to fight for to the end.

I take a deep breath. I know how to do this. I know how to play the game and win.

ANN CRAIG is a teacher, a mother, a friend, and a lover of literature. She lives in Texas with her three boisterous children, a beautiful Brittany spaniel (who is also himself quite a wild child), and a lovely cat who is the most popular member of her household. When she is not teaching, grading papers, and chasing or cleaning up after children, Ann spends her time laughing, playing board games, baking, and reading books.

FOR INDIGENOUS PEOPLES, ABORTION IS A RELIGIOUS RIGHT

ABAKI BECK AND ROSALYN LAPIER

After the Supreme Court reversed *Roe v. Wade* in June of 2022, Minnesota's Lt. Gov. Peggy Flanagan, a member of the White Earth Ojibwe Tribe, wrote on social media, "In Minnesota, your reproductive rights will stay protected. . . . Abortion is health care. Period." She wasn't just expressing the health care policy of Minnesota; she was also expressing the longstanding viewpoint of many Indigenous peoples. For thousands of years, reproductive health care has been an important part of Indigenous people's cultural practices, which include religious rituals, sacred rites, and the right to abortion.

With the ruling by the Supreme Court in *Dobbs v. Jackson Women's Health Organization*, a question emerges: To what extent will Indigenous religious and cultural practices related to reproductive health, including the right to an abortion, be impacted by this decision?

INDIGENOUS KNOWLEDGE
AND CEREMONY

Indigenous peoples have utilized the knowledge of medicinal plants throughout every stage of reproductive health care, from the start of menstruation to contraception, abortion, pregnancy, the birthing process, after birth, breastfeeding, uterine health, and menopause. Indigenous plant knowledge is passed down from generation to generation and is learned after years of formal training and by practicing proper cultural protocols. Our grandmother Annie Mad Plume Wall was a well-known and well-regarded Indigenous healer among the Blackfeet Nation of Montana. She learned plant knowledge from her grandmothers, including knowledge about reproductive health.

Our grandmother taught us that Blackfeet women used both medicinal plants and ritual practices for reproductive health. The Blackfeet used over a dozen plants to regulate menstruation, for abortion, for the birth process, and to address symptoms of menopause. Blackfeet women also held a religious ceremony during which a sanctified belt decorated with religious symbols was worn to regulate fertility and prevent pregnancy. Whether using medicinal plants or religious rituals, Blackfeet people viewed reproductive health and bodily autonomy as part of our relationship with the sacred realm.

RELIGIOUS VIEWPOINTS

While Christian conservatives viewed the recent decision as a "spiritual victory," not all religions view abortion the same. A Jewish synagogue in Southern Florida recently announced it was suing the state for violation of religious freedom after it passed a law restricting abortion. Islamic religious scholars assert that "classical Islamic law sees legal personhood as beginning at birth." Even Christian perspectives on abortion and contraceptive care have fluctuated over time and cultures, some religious studies scholars argue. In short: there is no single religious view of abortion.

The overturning of *Roe v. Wade* is part of a long legacy of American Christian values being forced on Indigenous communities. Indigenous peoples in the United States have only recently been able to assert their own religious ideas and practices. The American Indian Religious Freedom Act passed in 1978 after nearly 200 years of religious suppression by the United States government. This law guarantees that Indigenous people have a right to access religious sites, possess sacred objects, and have full freedom to worship and practice religious ceremonies. This includes reproductive health ceremonies.

Boarding schools run by Christian churches or the federal government also played a strong role in suppressing and criminalizing Native American cultures and religions. One impact that boarding schools had on Indigenous children and communities was loss of intergenerational cultural knowledge. The US government is just beginning to address part of this history as activists and members of Congress push for the passage of the Truth and Healing Commission on Indian Boarding School Policies Act.

REVITALIZATION OF INDIGENOUS KNOWLEDGE

Though Indigenous communities deeply suffered from the intentional destruction of our cultures and religions, there has been a vibrant resurgence in traditional ecological knowledge in our communities, including reproductive health care practices.

Indigenous people are revitalizing coming-of-age ceremonies that mark when someone begins menstruation, including Ojibwe berry fasts, a yearlong period in which young people abstain from eating berries and learn from their elders, and Hoopa Valley Tribal Flower Dance ceremonies, which Cutcha Risling Baldy, a professor of Native American studies at California State Polytechnic University, Humboldt, calls "a tangible, physical, spiritual and communal act of decolonization." Indigenous doulas and cultural birthing practices are also on the rise, with collectives popping up throughout Canada and the US.

In the days since the Supreme Court decision, several states with large tribal and urban Indian communities, including North Dakota, South Dakota, Wyoming, Idaho, and Oklahoma, have passed or introduced laws that ban or severely restrict abortion. Indigenous people on reservations seeking medical abortions or contraceptive care already face barriers; medical abortions and even Plan B pills are rarely available on reservation Indian Health Service facilities, where many Native people receive health care. The recent decision to overturn *Roe v. Wade* will likely exacerbate these barriers to Western health care.

What remains to be seen is how the decision and resulting state laws that ban abortion will exacerbate barriers to utilizing traditional medicinal practices and Indigenous knowledge—and if this is a violation of Indigenous people's centuries-old cultural and religious rights.

This article was originally published in YES! Magazine *on June 30, 2022, and is reprinted by permission of* YES!

ABAKI BECK is a public health graduate student and freelance writer. She writes about Indigenous feminism, Indigenous science and knowledge, and gender-based violence in Native communities.

ROSALYN LAPIER is an award-winning Indigenous writer, ethnobotanist, and environmental activist. She is the author of *Invisible Reality: Storytellers, Storytakers & the Supernatural World of the Blackfeet*. She is Blackfeet and Red River Métis.

NOT ALL RELIGIOUS PEOPLE

OPPOSE ABORTION

SARAH SELTZER

Nearly thirty years ago, my mother was one of the hundreds of thousands of people who attended the 1992 March for Women's Lives in Washington, DC. It was a pivotal moment for abortion rights at the Supreme Court, which was about to hear arguments in the case *Planned Parenthood v. Casey.* Though she left me at home, the words on her sign—"Every child a wanted child"—made an impression. So did the fact that the buses to Washington were chartered by our synagogue. When she returned, I wore the neon pink "Choice" hat she'd bought to my classroom at Jewish day school and began to spread the word.

That anecdote is not unique in the Jewish American experience: for many Jews, abortion rights are an ethical value, passed on from parent to child, with community support. The latest Pew Religious Landscape Study, from 2014, found that 83 percent of Jews surveyed supported legal abortion in most or all cases, more than any other religious group surveyed.

A firm commitment to abortion rights isn't just one of the socially liberal stances that progressive American Jews take. It's also a belief rooted in our sacred texts, which—despite differing interpretations across time and denominations—consistently prioritize the ultimate well-being of the pregnant person over that of the fetus.

That's why, as the right to an abortion has been decimated by a succession of state laws and the overturn of *Roe*, so many Jewish feminists are furious and ready for a fight.

Today when we think about faith and reproductive rights, it's easy to begin with the idea that religious groups oppose abortion. The modern anti-abortion movement, after all, arose as a coalition between conservative evangelicals and conservative Catholics.

But the Jewish stance is more complex, with roots in the Book of Exodus, where feticide is not treated as murder. The Talmud, where much of Jewish law is interpreted and where practice is hashed out, defines life as beginning when the baby's head emerges from the mother's body. Even in the once male-dominated rabbinate, the question of whose life takes precedence is clear.

"The principle in Jewish law is *tza'ar gufah kadim*, that her welfare is primary," wrote Rabbi David M. Feldman for the Conservative movement of Judaism back in 1983, referring to the pregnant person. "The fetus is unknown, future, potential, part of the 'secrets of God'; the mother is known, present, alive and asking for compassion."

Her welfare is primary. In Jewish tradition, the pregnant person's needs are central to the moral equation.

True, Orthodox Jews (and Orthodox Jewish organizations) are far more likely to take a political stand against abortion compared to Conservative, Reform, and Reconstructionist Jews. But in recent years, as when New York State liberalized its abortion law, Orthodox Jews were divided as much on gender as on politics on the question: interviewed by JTA, some Orthodox Jewish women expressed that they wanted the right to discuss the need for abortion with their rabbi and doctor, not with their political representatives.

As some Orthodox Jews have aligned themselves with the right on other issues, from Israel to immigration, so too have they moved toward the anti-abortion position. Still, even the strictest interpretation leaves room for the life of the mother. As Dr. Immanuel Jacobovits, an Orthodox rabbi, wrote in 1965, "as defined in the Bible, the rights of the mother and her unborn child are distinctly unequal, since the capital guilt of murder takes effect only if the victim was a born and viable person." That, he explained, doesn't mean abortion is never a grave offense, but "this inequality, then, is weighty enough only to warrant the sacrifice of the unborn child if the pregnancy otherwise poses a threat to the mother's life."

One of the core principles of Judaism is *pikuach nefesh*: the preservation of life above all else, even Shabbat observance, which is otherwise sacrosanct. What could be more worthy than focusing on the need for the pregnant person, if suffering, to end that suffering, to live and contribute to the world? It is her life, her soul—"present, alive, and asking for compassion," as Rabbi Feldman put it—that is more worth saving.

We are far from the only religion to take a nuanced stance on abortion. But a religious group that dictates a sweeping, intractable view of right and wrong when it comes to abortion may have an easier time getting attention than, for instance, the religious organizations that recently filed an amicus brief to the Supreme Court asking fervently for careful, circumstance-based consideration in the upcoming abortion case out of Mississippi.

And so a number of Jews are starting to make noise to rectify this imbalance. A new campaign called 73Forward, led by the National Council of Jewish Women, is gathering activists from secular to Orthodox to defend abortion access from an explicitly Jewish perspective. Rabbis have pledged to join the fight in Texas.

Feminist organizing has always attracted Jewish participation, while within our communal world, groups like the NCJW and publications like *Lilith* (organizations where I worked and now work, respectively) have carried the abortion rights banner for many years. But what is notable today are the particular ways Jews are organizing as Jews.

Gen Z and millennial Jewish leaders also point to the reproductive justice movement led by women of color—which connects abortion to racial, economic, and social inequality— as the beacon for their own activism. This holistic framework has inspired Jews to fight for abortion access as a crucial part of repairing the world, or *tikkun olam,* a value that has animated Jewish activism for decades. Many Jewish feminists say they now feel called to support abortion access for those who need it the most, while reminding the country that our own religious freedom is at stake.

Jewish leaders aren't on television each weekend screaming, "Get your laws off our religion!" But as a minority religion, we naturally favor a true separation of church and state. And there's another reason. When I write about Jewish attitudes toward contraception or abortion, I always receive an onslaught of vitriol in my inbox. It starts with the horrifying comparison between abortion and the Holocaust that equates millions of thinking, feeling, Jewish lives cut down in their prime to embryos, and extends to the idea that 83 percent of American Jews in support of abortion rights are perpetuating the very mass murder that devastated my grandparents' generation.

Harassment facing Jews who support abortion often goes back to one of the oldest lies in antisemitic history: the lie that Jewish people ritually sacrifice children. This trope, known as blood libel, has historically posed mortal danger to members of our community. In 1990 an article by my colleague Susan Weidman Schneider at *Lilith* detailed a disturbing trend: the increasing use of antisemitism in fliers distributed by people harassing abortion clinics. The piece noted how intrinsic the trope of the Jewish abortion doctor profiting off innocent blood was to the zealous anti-choice movement of that era. It was a sadly prescient observation. In 1998, Dr. Barnett Slepian was murdered after returning home from synagogue, where he was praying for his dead father. In a world where many hate us for who we are, it may be daunting for Jews to speak out instead of blending in.

But regardless of potential backlash, this moment is perilous for religious and bodily freedom, and it calls for courage. "There is a loud group of people using faith as a weapon. We can't stand by and let that happen," says the NCJW's CEO, Sheila Katz. She's right. As my mom's old protest sign reminds us, reproductive rights—including abortion—give us the chance to create families, and individual futures, that are wanted, cherished, and loved. What value is more Jewish than that?

"Not All Religious People Oppose Abortion," by Sarah Seltzer, originally appeared in The New York Times *on November 18, 2021. It has been updated to account for the overturning of* Roe v. Wade.

***

SARAH SELTZER is an editor at *Lilith*, a feminist Jewish magazine.

THE BEAUTIFUL SCREAM

LISA SHARON HARPER

In her 2022 book, Fortune: How Race Broke My
Family and the World—and How to Repair It All,
*activist and public theologian Lisa Sharon Harper
dives into ten generations of her family history,
unmasking the impact of race on the lives of those
who came before her—and on her own life. During
the turbulent period of her adolescent years, as she
struggled to deal with her mother's depression, a
newly merged step-family, and merciless bullying in
school, Lisa found safety in white evangelical youth
groups, which shaped her early thinking about a
range of issues, including abortion.*

*In this passage, an excerpt from her book, Lisa
describes the indoctrination she received as part of
her participation in anti-abortion groups in college,
and the startling confrontation with her mother to
which it led.*

—EH

Throughout my junior and senior years at Rutgers University, pro-life and pro-choice rallies proliferated across the New Brunswick campus. I attended pro-life rallies with my friends in Campus Crusade for Christ. Unfamiliar with the debate, I hung back on the edges, watching the mostly white crowd scream and chant. We felt important, like we were part of something bigger than ourselves, though I hardly understood what I was chanting for. Peppered throughout the speeches from the stage, speaker after speaker merely confirmed that abortion was wrong. Pictures of aborted fetuses plastered to picket signs waved as women and men stepped to the microphone and talked about the fetus's silent scream.

Two years after hosting a viewing of the 1972 cult classic *A Thief in the Night*, my Campus Crusade chapter sponsored a viewing of the 1984 agitprop film *The Silent Scream*, which debuted on Jerry Falwell's televangelist program. The room was packed with students silenced to a hush when Dr. Bernard Nathanson's narration interpreted the ultrasound of an abortion of a twelve-week-old fetus: "We can see the child moving rather serenely in the uterus." Nathanson characterizes the fetus as fully aware, able to sense danger and respond: "The child senses aggression in its sanctuary." Nathanson then imprints on the minds of viewers an image paralleled only by Edvard Munch's painting *The Scream*: "We see the child's mouth wide open in a silent scream." I will never forget it. It was like a horror movie. It was that image and the interpretation of the fetus's movement that tapped my deepest cry for justice and moved me to march "for life."

But four years before I marched and before my Campus Crusade chapter showed this film, *CBS Morning*

News had sat down with five physicians recommended by the American College of Obstetricians and Gynecologists for their expertise in ultrasound analysis and fetal development to analyze that part of the film. The physicians explained that the cerebral cortex, the part of the brain that perceives pain, isn't functioning yet at twelve weeks. It's just not a factor. It's impossible that the fetus felt anything. So why did the video show the fetus suddenly thrash about? Because moments before the thrashing, the filmmaker slowed the film down to a crawl's pace. Then, just as the catheter suction tube is placed, the filmmaker turned the speed to regular pace.

Pro-life "experts" tried to rebut the physicians' analysis, but they couldn't. Instead, they dug in deeper. They admitted the cerebral cortex is not developed and minimized the fallacy by saying the abortion issue is not about pain. Oh, but *The Silent Scream* is all about pain. That's the entire point. The filmmaker intentionally misled viewers. He intentionally misled me. No one ever shared that CBS report with me. No one ever shared the testimonies of obstetricians. Instead, they showed the film to a room full of college students. They made young jaws drop with false testimony. Doctors who disagreed were demonized as "liberal." Then they gave us an opportunity to march.

One day that year, my mother and I stumbled into a heated argument. Exasperated, I bent backward to convince her that her pro-choice position was immoral and un-Christian.

She asked, "What if the life of the mother is at stake? Should abortion be allowed then?"

"No," I countered flatly. I believed God was supreme. If God willed that the mother die, who am I to argue with God? I did not realize that was the exact same logic that the evangelical church used to justify slavery: If God ordained certain people to be slaves, who are we to argue with God?

"Lisa," my mother explained, "do you remember that time I was pregnant a few years ago, and I went into the hospital and the baby didn't make it?"

"Yes . . ." I scowled.

"I had an abortion," she said.

My heart stopped.

"I almost died, and the doctor had to take the baby to save my life." She paused. "I could have died."

I stood before my mother, a good Christian soldier. I was determined to win. With a heart of steel, I looked my mother in the eyes—my mother, the woman who almost died to bring me into the world, who worked nights to put herself through college while raising three small children, who would give up anything to make sure we were provided for—and I said, "They should have saved the baby."

Excerpt from Fortune *by Lisa Sharon Harper, copyright © 2022. Used by permission of Brazos Press, a division of Baker Publishing Group.*

Today, as an activist and religious leader, Lisa works to promote racial equity, economic inclusion, and gender justice in communities of all kinds. This includes efforts to engage evangelicals in public conversations on the issue of abortion. I asked Lisa to share her perspective on what the work to destigmatize abortion can look like within faith communities, and what follows is her powerful response to that request.

—EH

Several years ago, I launched a pilgrimage designed to help Christian women (mostly evangelical) connect with and understand their place in our national and ecclesial struggles for women's equality. The RubyWooPilgrimage (named after the fiery red MAC lipstick color) rolls through the fabled Seneca Falls origin story of the women's rights movement; through New York City's diverse panoply of historic immigrant women leaders; through Atlantic City, where Fannie Lou Hamer told the 1964 Democratic Convention she wept for America. There, we consider the power of women in elected office. The journey concludes with a lobby day on Capitol Hill.

In 2019, the Pilgrimage dared to do something we had never seen done before: talk openly about abortion in a diverse group of Christian women.

Our twenty-five women leaders, writers, pastors, and theologians from every corner of the US sat around circular tables at a private dinner generously hosted by Auburn Seminary. We talked, laughed, and remembered our time in Seneca Falls earlier that day.

Then Rev. Susan Chorley, cofounder of Exhale ProVoice, patched into our gathering via Zoom and shared her abortion story.

It struck me that I had never heard a Christian woman, let alone a pastor, talk about her own abortion—ever. The assumption is that Christian women don't have abortions.

I asked the women: "Who here has ever had a conversation in public or private about abortion before tonight?"

No one raised their hand.

I marveled. How is it possible that so many Christians, especially evangelicals, have made the issue of abortion the single driver of their vote without ever even talking about the issue—not even in private?

I asked our assembly of leaders to go into their table

groups and share the story of the first time they ever learned that abortion was an issue.

Nearly all of the women said they first learned that abortion was an issue when they started attending a white evangelical church.

Then I asked the women to share the story of their own intersection with the issue of abortion, whether through friends or family or through their own personal experience.

The air in the room became tender. Women leaned in and spoke from deep, untapped places. They told stories they had never told before—stories of pain, confusion, relief, and rage at how they were treated by their churches. Women had been shunned by their churches both for terminating pregnancies and for being unable to have children.

Tears of rage and release flowed as the women shared their stories with the larger group. I shared the story of my words to my mother.

As we closed our time, both fury and sorrow coursed between us. We had allowed our voices and our stories to be controlled and silenced by white patriarchy inside the church.

The only way to break free was to use our voices.

So, on the count of three, we closed our time by breaking our silence with a primal scream that threatened to shatter the glass panel windows that surrounded us.

On the other side of that beautiful scream was liberation.

LISA SHARON HARPER is a writer, activist, and public theologian. President and founder of FreedomRoad.us, Lisa is also author of several books, including the critically acclaimed *Fortune: How Race Broke My Family and the World—and How to Repair It All* and *The Very Good Gospel*.

"EVERY SINGLE ONE OF THEM RESPONDED IN TEARS"

A Q&A WITH ROBIN MARTY, WEST ALABAMA WOMEN'S CENTER

As someone who works on the front lines of abortion care in the US, Robin Marty knows better than most what the loss of Roe *will mean for the lives of everyday people. Robin serves as Director of Operations for the West Alabama Women's Center in Tuscaloosa, Alabama, and is the author of two books on reproductive rights:* A New Handbook for a Post-Roe America *and* The End of Roe v. Wade.

In this interview, Robin shares the story of how Dobbs *impacted life at her Alabama clinic even before the Supreme Court ruled, as well as what happened once news broke that* Roe *had officially been struck down. The interview has been edited for clarity and length.*

—EH

ELIZABETH HINES: You started out as a freelance journalist, and now you're the author of the essential abortion resource guide *A New Handbook for a Post- Roe America.* What moved you to start writing about abortion?

ROBIN MARTY: I grew up in Nebraska, and I'd always been rebelliously liberal and in favor of abortion rights as a child. When I moved to Minnesota after I graduated college, I ended up working for an investment banking firm—and it was soul-sucking. This was right after George W. Bush won his first term, and it kind of soured me on world politics, because *Bush v. Gore* was such a horrible case. So, I started writing a political blog then, and that eventually led me to progressive activism.

But it was after the 2008 Obama election that I really started to track the different pieces of model legislation restricting abortion that were coming out at the state level and that nobody was paying attention to. It was very clear that something was going on nationally, that started at a state level, to try to end abortion rights by provoking a challenge to *Roe v. Wade.* This crystallized for me right after the Affordable Care Act fight, which was a battle where Democrats held the White House and a House majority and a Senate majority, and somehow we still got a watered-down health care plan that eliminated access to abortion in the insurance plans.

This mattered a lot to me because at the moment that amendment was introduced, I was in the hospital having a D&C for a miscarriage. It was my second pregnancy and it was a very wanted pregnancy. When I went in for a twelve-week checkup, I found out that the embryo hadn't made it past the eighth week. Even though I had been writing about abortion rights as one of the parts of progressive activism in general, and even though I'd been following the health care fight, this was the moment where I finally understood, personally, what it was like to need an abortion. Because while my surgery was covered by insurance, as soon as I learned that I would need a D&C, I realized very quickly that my doctor couldn't perform one because he hadn't been trained how.

EH: That sounds terrifying. What did you do?

RM: I think it says a lot about the stigma around abortion in our country that it never occurred to me that I could go to a Planned Parenthood and get care, or that I could go to the local abortion clinic and get care. Instead, I spent the rest of the day calling doctors, trying to find somebody that was covered by my insurance who would let me come in and have this surgery. Eventually, I had to go to a hospital to do it.

It was on Halloween that I ended up having the procedure with a new doctor I'd never seen before. But during that period in between, I had something inside me that I could not remove, that had essentially taken over my entire life, and I could not do anything about it without a doctor's permission. That was the point at which it really, finally occurred to me that this is what people may feel when they have an unwanted pregnancy, whatever that unwanted pregnancy circumstance is. I mean, my insurance coded it as abortion. That's what they called it in the hospital. A D&C for a miscarriage is really not different. It's the same procedure. It's the same crashing of hormones. It's the same moment where you cannot move forward in your life until this is taken care of. You are pregnant and you cannot not be pregnant until this is done. It's the same thing. The only difference was that my pregnancy was wanted, and another person's pregnancy may not be. That was what galvanized me toward abortion rights.

I spent the next decade tracking model anti-abortion bills for RH Reality Check (now Rewire News) and I wrote my first book, which explained the ten different ways the Supreme Court could possibly overturn *Roe v. Wade* based on the model legislation that was coming out. It was 2013, and we had an entire blueprint of exactly what the Right was going to do—and everyone ignored us. That was what kept me going.

EH: A few years ago you decided to transition from solely writing about abortion to working in the provider space yourself. Now you're the director of operations for the West Alabama Women's Center. What was daily life at your clinic like before *Roe* fell?

RM: [Before SCOTUS overturned *Roe*,] West Alabama Women's Center was responsible for about half of the abortions in the state of Alabama. It was the largest clinic in the state, and it's been around since the early 1990s. Before 2022, what we typically saw was about 200 patients a month, the vast majority of them being from Alabama and maybe a few patients from Mississippi. They were primarily Black women and I'd say about two-thirds were already parents. Many of them were either uninsured or on Medicaid. Medicaid did not cover abortions. Most of them were working multiple jobs or were home with multiple children.

These were people who were already having a difficult time accessing any sort of health care, especially preventative health care like birth control. A number of people came in because either they were denied the type of birth control that they wanted from their doctors, or they were in some other way unable to access it because county health departments had such a backup in appointments that they couldn't get in for the birth control that they actually wanted to use, and they couldn't afford the other options of seeing a private doctor or getting it from online sources.

So, these were the patients we were seeing. A typical day would be between five and ten first-trimester procedures in the morning, and then we would do medication abortions in the afternoon. That was how things were until 2022—which was how long it took for the wave of people who were coming from Texas to finally make it over to Alabama. During this period, we saw that Mississippi patients were being pushed out of their clinics and over into our state because Mississippi was too full, because Louisiana patients were being pushed over to Mississippi because Louisiana clinics were closed. And Texas patients were coming in because they didn't have any closer clinics either.

This wave just kept moving its way farther and farther over until, as of June of 2022, we were seeing 300 to 350 patients in a month. Probably 30 percent of them were from out of state. It was still primarily the same demographic, but people were coming from farther distances. We were seeing more people who were needing assistance with hotels and with gas in order to help them make this trek.

EH: Tell me about when the ruling came down. What was that moment like for you and the patients at your clinic?

RM: I was actually on *Headline News* the moment the decision came down. I'd decided that I would do an interview—a live interview—because we thought there wasn't going to be a decision on *Dobbs* that day; we'd assumed that *Dobbs* would be the absolute last decision they handed down. In the middle of the interview, my phone started going off. When it wouldn't stop, I checked Twitter, where the SCOTUS blog was up, and saw what had happened. I looked back into the screen and told the anchors that *Roe v. Wade* had just been overturned, and I needed to leave. I picked up my phone and walked out of the frame and called the clinic's staff to tell them to stop seeing patients immediately.

We had twenty-one patients in our waiting room that day. These were all patients who were in for ultrasounds to start the clock ticking on the forty-eight-hour waiting period mandated by the state of Alabama. Nobody was in for an abortion that day because our provider had been called away on a family emergency. And every single one of them, when they were told, responded in tears. People had no idea what they were going to do next.

Luckily, we had a process in place, so we were ready for this part. Since we knew the decision was coming sooner or later, we had made an agreement with another clinic to send patients to a state where abortion was still going to be legal. Ultimately, we were able to fund first-day appointments for these patients and then also help them with any additional travel expenses they might need so they could get there—because now they were going to have to travel at least another three-and-a-half hours. Like I said, many of these patients weren't even from Alabama to start with. This is the process that we've been working through since that day, and have just now finished, which involves supporting the 100 or so patients we had booked for the last week of June, but we can't see. And the phone still keeps ringing. That's where we are.

EH: What worries you the most about where we now stand relative to abortion rights?

RM: I think the biggest worry that everyone else has right now is this idea that people are going to die seeking out illegal abortions. I don't think that's true at all. Abortion in itself is obviously far safer than childbirth, and also, we know that there are safe places, nationally and internationally, to obtain vetted pills that are the same medication that we provide in our clinic. We know that in states like ours the people who receive them are going to be in a murky legal area and that their families could be under suspicion, but the actual act of an abortion is not going to be dangerous for the most part, and that gives me a lot of relief.

We keep talking about how dangerous a post-*Roe* America will be physically, but the reality is that the real danger is going to be for every person who remains pregnant. In Alabama, we have not expanded Medicaid. There is very little access to contraception to start with. Our hospitals are overloaded, and many have very, very poor quality. Our state's maternal mortality rate is, I believe, 33 out of 10,000 live births. It's the third highest in the country. People here get abortions not just because they feel they can't raise a child but because they are scared to give birth. These are people who are now going to have less healthy pregnancies, people who likely have not been able to access prenatal care because they were trying to find ways to access an abortion. Once you add that to our very racist medical system, especially out here, we are looking at poor health outcomes both for those people who are pregnant and for their children, if they do have them.

That's the part that worries me the most. It's not, "Will they hurt themselves trying to get a medication abortion?"— it's, "Are they going to forego the abortion, try to give birth, and then die that way?"

EH: You're pretty much the guru of what we should do to protect ourselves in post-*Roe* America. So what should people who want to take action do right now?

RM: I know we talk a lot about voting, and voting is very important, obviously, but I think the most important thing to do right now is to be as vocal as possible about the entire direction that the country is taking. I think that if this last session of the Supreme Court has taught us anything, it's that all precedent is gone—that all the things that we have thought in the past were settled constitutional rights are now back on the table and up for grabs. We've already seen Clarence Thomas discuss how he thinks *Griswold v. Connecticut* was wrongly decided, which means that birth control for all people is going to be the next thing that could potentially disappear. We know that they're already making noises about the end of gay marriage. Everybody's rights are in some way, shape, or form back up for debate, except for those of white cis males, and that should make everybody scared.

We know that a majority of people do not support these laws, these rules, these intentions. So, we have to get loud in every area. Not just in voting, but in the media and in protests. Get loud and make sure there are letters to the editors. Get loud in going back and speaking up when there are legislators who have open hearing sessions about their laws. We need to be protesting every new bill that happens in our state legislatures. We need to get involved at the most local levels in our county elections and city elections. We have to be as engaged and loud as possible because we were quiet—and being quiet let them take over large chunks of this country. If we don't reverse that immediately, the next thing we're going to be looking at is a federal abortion ban.

EH: Is there anything in your work right now that gives you hope?

RM: Yes. I'm actually ridiculously hopeful right now. I know that sounds confounding considering where we are sitting, but here's the reality: abortion was already something that was very hard to get in Alabama and that was extraordinarily needed—and it's going to be even more needed now that it's not legal here. But all reproductive health care is scarce out here, especially when it comes to STI testing, HIV care, trans health care, even prenatal care and annual exams.

If there is any silver lining in this right now, it's the fact that by no longer feeling obligated to deal with the flood of patients that have been coming into our state, we will be able to take the time—if we can stay open and if we can find a source of funding—to start offering all of these other essential resources. We've already had our first prenatal appointments. We are already seeing patients for PrEP. We have three IUD appointments scheduled for this week. All of these other aspects of care are so necessary—just as much as abortion care was. If there's no other bright side to this, it's that now we have the time to build those programs and market those programs and make sure that the people who need this care can find it.

EH: Is there anything else people need to understand about the future of reproductive justice in America? Where do we go from here?

RM: I want to make sure that people look closely at how we are resourcing this fight. I've seen a lot of people discussing what a post-*Roe* America will look like, especially if we remain in these divided states, and there seems to be a focus on making sure people can leave their states to get an abortion somewhere else; making sure that "haven states" have all these extra clinics and extra people and extra money.

One of the things I ask people to do is examine how there's some inherent racism in that approach. Because the idea is to resource all of these blue states, which are mostly white states, while abandoning the southern states, where the highest proportion of Black Americans live.

This is so important to recognize, because if we as a movement truly believe that abortion is a human right and bodily autonomy belongs to each person, then it shouldn't matter where a person gets an abortion, where a person lives, their race, their age—any of these things. What should matter is that they are able to access it in the way that's easiest for them, and that they have the means to help them do that. If we're only focusing on getting people out of red states and into blue states in order to get care, we're always going to be leaving behind the most marginalized—because there are people who are never going to have enough money, or support, or wherewithal to go through all the logistics necessary to leave their states to access this care.

In short, we need to continue to invest just as heavily in red states now as we did when abortion was legal, and to support the groups that are deep in the communities here. We must trust these groups enough to take their word that they have found a means to do the work in the most effective way possible—even if they may not be able to share publicly exactly what these actions entail. Black people have always found a way to create their families regardless of the oppressions they have faced or the laws that have existed, and they will continue to do so in the face of these new challenges.

Invest in clinics that are still here and will care for those who manage their own abortions. Invest in abortion funds that provide full reproductive justice support and trust they will make sure pregnant people can get what they need. We will always be here to help.

ROBIN MARTY is Director of Operations for West Alabama Women's Center in Tuscaloosa, Alabama. She is the author of *A New Handbook for a Post-Roe America* and *The End of Roe v. Wade*. Her work can be found at *Time* magazine, NBC, *Cosmopolitan*, *Politico*, *Rolling Stone* and more.

CLINIC

ALISSA QUART

1.
When we type "abortion"
autofill writes, *I am pregnant.*
I am pregnant in
Spanish. I am having
a baby and have no
insurance. I'm scared of having
a baby. What trimester am I
What trimester is abortion illegal?
Google says: *I need your love.*
I need an abortion.
I am pregnant can I eat shrimp?
Am I having a miscarriage?
I need help paying for abortion.
Abortion clinic violence.
Not ready to have this baby.

2.
God will punish, old ones
say in unison. They sing,

"Genocide." A man
with a Santa beard and a long gun
enters a clinic in Indiana.
In Mississippi, it's day-glo
signs, floppy hats, tiny
peachy fetus dolls.
Their lawn chairs
too near Women's Health,
their flesh sunscreen white.
Metal-detectors-
as-framing-devices.
Surveillance cameras as
glass birds.
In a place like this, in America, a long gun.
Women afraid of dying while
they are trying to find their life.

3.
On a normal day, women aged
23, 19, 41, 35.
Work at Kmart, Home Depot,
at daycares, at the hospitals
at night. Today, they learn
a new vocabulary.
Ultrasound, waiting period,
Trailways, TRAP law,
witnesses. They learn
the way euphemisms mostly tell
the truth. That the polite
word is always "discomfort."
The door clicks when it locks.
Hungry to talk, no words.

4.
She's got a cold from
her two-year-old.
The doctor talks through
the procedure. The someone
holding her hand, not
her husband.
From a Baptist town, her mother
full of God. So she lied,
got on the bus here. Drove
for three hours, borrowed
money for the hooker
motel, then the overnight
waiting period. Wondered whether
God cared or was it the care
her mother managed.
One girl was a sturdy teenager,
tall enough to play center.
Signed the parental notification
with a broken ballpoint.
Another, redheaded, the hottest
number at the Bingo Hall in
Shreveport. Grandma drank.
"What about your boyfriend?"
She answers, "He stopped
talking to me. All he wanted
was the baby."
With her own body, hurtling.
One boss wouldn't let
the woman sell car parts
if she was pregnant.
One minister called
the clinic "baby parts."
One was doing this *for*

the other baby.
The soldier said she was
doing this *so I can fight*
for this country.

5.
The ATM spits $500.
She slid inside the office
building, paid money to
a counter lady, was led into
a paneled private
room, Reagan-era
red, with fake curtains,
a bad stage set.
Silk fishtail fern,
mustard satin bedspread.
She was put to sleep
woke up to saltines,
other posh sleepy women
in gowns, a cultic circle.
Her friend called it
"The Anaconda."
Always the code
words and then the surprise
guiltlessness.

6.
Bed rest with the mysteries. Old blood.
A mandala of succor and suffering.
Dark blood could mean anything.
It gets sloppy when you are trying to find love.
A glass of water, a small
pill. Hard candy, saltines
afterwards. Silk
flower in your hair.

7.
Poems about abortion,
poems about abortion and feelings
of sorrow. Google says: *shame or guilt;*
Remorse is Forever: Abortion Poem.
Post Abortion Stress Syndrome
Support. Poems about abortion from
a baby's point of view.

8.
Say: No shame.
We can say: The
birth spectrum.
Choices are always field work,
freedom song, elegy,
captivity narrative.
This feeling won't forget them;
won't forget you.

This poem is a part of Alissa Quart's collection Thoughts and Prayers, *published in 2019 by OR Books.*

ALISSA QUART is the executive director of the Economic Hardship Reporting Project. She is the author of the poetry collections *Thoughts and Prayers* and *Monetized* as well as four nonfiction books, most recently, *Squeezed: Why Our Families Can't Afford America*. She has also executive produced or worked on numerous nonfiction projects about abortion, including the Emmy-winning documentary *Jackson*, *The Last Clinic*, and *Reconception*. Her poems have been published in *Granta* and *The Nation*, among other publications, and her journalism has appeared in many publications, among them *The New York Times* and *The Washington Post*.

MY TRIP TO TEXAS GAVE
ME A GLIMPSE INTO
THE POST-*ROE* FUTURE

ROSA VALDERRAMA

First, let's dispense with the bullshit. Abortion is health care; that is not open to debate. Abortion care is part of a spectrum of reproductive health care that, like prenatal care, birth care, postpartum care, cancer screenings, fibroid treatments, and endometriosis care, must be available to all our communities with dignity and self-determination. Abortion carries more shame and stigma than the rest of these reproductive health services, but if we're honest, we can acknowledge that there is still plenty of shame and stigma surrounding other reproductive health issues, like periods, miscarriages, and sexually transmitted infections (STIs).

Plus, access to abortion care is a fundamental human right, full stop. No court or politician should dictate who among us can have children, when, how many, or under what circumstances. Forcing a person to remain pregnant and give birth against their will is a gross violation of our human rights and dignity. Everyone has the fundamental human right to decide if and how they want to become a parent, and when they want to build and grow their own families.

No one understands that better than the Poderosas in the Rio Grande Valley of Texas, a sprawling region along the southern border with about a million inhabitants, most of them with close cultural, if not family, ties to Mexico.

Although some folks know the RGV as a conservative, rural stretch of Texas, home to Mexican im/migrants and their descendants, the RGV I saw firsthand this year is a vibrant force of power, a beam of resistance to the state's forced-birth agenda.

That's where the Poderosas come in. *Poderosa* means "empowered woman" or "powerful one" in Spanish. It's what the National Latina Institute for Reproductive Justice (Latina Institute) activists have gone by for decades. I started out as a Poderosa activist where I live in Florida before I joined the communications staff at the Latina Institute.

The Poderosas organize around reproductive health, rights, and justice issues. They take part in leadership trainings, lobby their elected officials, canvas their neighborhoods—not for a politician, but around questions of reproductive justice—and organize rallies, health fairs, and other local events to benefit their communities.

Many of them don't have the proper documentation to live and work in this country, but that doesn't stop them from fighting for their communities. For years, US Customs and Border Protection (CBP) has set up random checkpoints along most major routes in Southern Texas, blocking undocumented people from traveling to the next town, let alone out of the state, to seek care.

In March of 2022, I traveled to Brownsville to celebrate the fifteenth anniversary of the Latina Institute Texas's organizing work in the Valley. Their *quince* also marked six months since the state enacted what was then the most extreme abortion ban in the country. In September 2021, SB 8 went into effect, banning abortion care in Texas after six weeks of pregnancy, or just one missed period, which is before many people even realize they're pregnant.

Texas has been ground zero for the war on abortion access and reproductive rights. We are now seeing that battle play out across the country after a highly partisan Supreme Court overturned nearly fifty years of settled law with its ruling on *Dobbs v. Jackson Women's Health Organization*. In this post-*Roe* landscape, Kansas voters showed us that abortion is not just a left-wing issue, it's something everyone cares about.

The only saving grace of our post-*Roe* reality is that nobody knows what's next, and that means anything is possible. Now is the time to make things happen. Now is the time to share information about self-managed medication abortion care with mifepristone and misoprostol or misoprostol alone. Let's talk about how safe it is, how effective and accessible it can be. Let's make sure everyone knows about PlanCpills.org and AidAccess.org.

I refuse to let any court or politician force me to become a parent against my will, and so should you. There is no more egregious violation of a person's human rights than forced pregnancy and birth.

While a dozen states have banned abortion care altogether since the Supreme Court overturned *Roe v. Wade*, Florida is dealing with a fifteen-week ban on abortion care enacted before the *Dobbs* decision. Governor Ron DeSantis has vowed to sign any and all anti-abortion legislation, and the state legislature has consistently voted against the will of the people of Florida, who overwhelmingly support abortion access, to enforce baseless restrictions on a safe, normal, health care procedure.

As these restrictions creep across our country, we must look to the people of Texas—not just the Poderosas but also the entire community of activists who contribute their time and energy to the dynamic network of abortion funds, human-rights organizations, and reproductive-justice coalitions in the area. The RGV is home to the Frontera Fund, which provides financial and practical support to folks seeking abortion care, and South Texans for Reproductive Justice (STRJ), which has been working ceaselessly on a campaign to provide Plan B emergency contraception to anyone who needs it in the Valley.

Everyone I met during my trip to Texas was an inspiration, from the Poderosas who led the event to celebrate Latina Institute Texas's fifteen years of organizing to the young activists who followed their mothers into the movement. I'll never forget running over in a panic to warn the young parents whose kids were going hard at the SB 8 piñatas that the piñatas also had prizes in them: care packages with emergency contraception donated by STRJ. One mom simply smiled at me and calmly handed me one of the packages she had retrieved from her kids. I asked her if she knew someone who could use it, and she nodded and put it back in her purse.

The moment was incredibly significant. As one Poderosa said during a filmed interview taken at the event, "Reproductive health care and reproductive justice isn't really talked about within my community. There are so many of my friends who I've had to teach what reproductive justice and health care is, and they sometimes feel embarrassed because these are rights that people should know ... As a member of the newer generation, I would say, hear our voices, listen to us, and take into consideration what we are saying."

The organizers and activists of the Rio Grande Valley are truly unstoppable, and we must look to them to lead the way to fight for our human rights and work toward reproductive justice.

During the few days I spent with them in March, I saw a multigenerational coalition of compassionate, joyful people. I interviewed over a dozen Poderosas who have been activists with Latina Institute Texas for many years about their experiences organizing in the Valley. Many of them were joined at the rally by their sisters, daughters, mothers, sons, mothers-in-law, and even grandmothers. It was an amazing sight to see. In the video, when one activist present was asked what it meant to be a Poderosa, she replied, "It means I can mobilize communities, raise my voice, and let people know that all of us have rights."

This is what the resistance looks like. Watch it yourself and steel your resolve, because we are in for a big fight.

To watch the video of the Poderosas of Texas, visit:
https://bit.ly/PoderosasNLI

This piece is published by permission of the author and Vox Media, LLC, and was originally published on June 21, 2022 at www.popsugar.com/fitness/poderosas -abortion-rights-activism-essay-48854965. It has been updated to reflect the Supreme Court's overturning of Roe v. Wade.

ROSA VALDERRAMA is the communications director at Asylum Seeker Advocacy Project (ASAP) and a board member at the Broward Women's Emergency Fund. She previously headed the communications department at the National Latina Institute for Reproductive Justice.

THE PRIVILEGE OF HOPE:
WORKING IN PARTNERSHIP
WITH YOUNG PEOPLE

TAMARA MARZOUK

In 2017, I was working as a school social worker speaking to high school students about how common abortion is in the United States. "Can you imagine if one of us in this room had had an abortion?" a student said, and laughed. I paused and responded with, "You never know," and reminded them again just how many people in this country have abortions.

By that point, I had been advising young people on pregnancy options for years. I had had an abortion myself. But I almost never talked about my own abortion publicly; stigma and shame played their part in keeping so many of us, myself included, silenced. And then one day, while I was working with youth activists, I listened as a young woman named Lea shared her abortion story. In the middle of an Abortion 101 training, she offered an example from her own abortion experiences. She spoke courageously about the systemic barriers she'd encountered and the range of emotions that had accompanied her experience. After she spoke, I watched as another young person was moved to volunteer their story. That day, I witnessed the snowball effect of story sharing, and I felt energized with hope that I, too, could share my story more openly as time went on.

Lea and other youth activists with whom I work, some as young as eighteen, identify as abortion storytellers and they speak about their abortions publicly—to the press, to policy makers, and on social media—to help destigmatize abortion care. Their vulnerability, their willingness to share this part of themselves, challenged and inspired me to do the same.

My abortion took place six years before we lost *Roe*, but so many barriers already existed to accessing care. The experience was rarely discussed without shame and stigma. For some people, the nearest provider was hundreds of miles away. Across the country, invasive, medically unnecessary restrictions already existed in dozens of states. We didn't know we'd lose *Roe*—but in some parts of the country, and especially for youth, low-income people, and people of color, access to abortion had already been decimated.

I found out I was pregnant right after I earned my graduate degree, and I knew I didn't want to be. For me, making the decision to have an abortion was the easy part. What came after was far more complex. I naively thought that because I had spent years as a sex educator, school social worker, and pregnancy options counselor, I might be immune to the fear of stigma and shame that I witnessed in so many others. But I wasn't. Even with the support of my partner and multiple friends, I worried about who to tell and how often I should share.

When I was seeking an abortion, I also incorrectly assumed that my campus health center could help me. They just told me to call Planned Parenthood. I couldn't believe that an institution as large as my university, which offered students services for every other kind of health care situation imaginable, couldn't support me in accessing an abortion. While I had heard about barriers like these through the young people I had worked with in direct service, I now felt firsthand the lack of institutional support for my abortion care, even in a state with few abortion restrictions in place.

Yet even with those barriers, I know that my abortion experience was comparatively easy—especially now that our Constitutional right to abortion has been wiped out. It sickens me to think of anyone becoming pregnant without the option of abortion. Being able to get an abortion allowed me to work for the future and the life I wanted—a right every person deserves to have access to.

But the simple truth is, that is not the nation we live in today; every person does not have equal access to that right. We know that restricting abortion is racist, sexist, and cissexist. It is also ageist. Young people are disproportionately impacted by abortion restrictions due to inability to travel long distances, afford prohibitive costs, and take time off of school and work. Abortion bans of any kind contribute to a culture of policing in the United States, and restrict bodily autonomy. We know that young people; Black, Indigenous, and other people of color; system-involved, disabled, undocumented, trans, and gender-expansive communities; and those who have trouble making ends meet are more likely to be criminalized simply because of the bodies they live in. Young people recognize and honor this truth, and they work toward a new reality despite the discriminatory challenges they face.

My own abortion experience and my career centering young people's agency in reproductive decision-making have led me to work with young people who are fighting for abortion access for all people, but especially for their peers. I am now Director of Youth Abortion Access at Advocates for Youth, a national nonprofit that supports youth activists ages fourteen to twenty-four across the country who are working to secure reproductive health, rights, and justice for all. Working alongside young people, I have the privilege of feeling hopeful every single day. I witness creativity, joy, and collaboration, coupled with the pain of working in the abortion movement at this particular moment in time. I have been inspired to join young people sharing their abortion stories as a form of advocacy. If it wasn't for their example, I don't know that I would be writing this piece today.

No matter what happens with abortion policy at the state and federal levels, young people will not let the right to abortion access go away. They engage in the fight for abortion access in so many ways. They support one another through sharing information about abortion access and about self-managed abortion; they welcome one another with open arms into the community of abortion activists; they approach one another with care and curiosity. They fly across the country to support their fellow activists who work in areas more hostile to abortion. The Youth Abortion Support Collective is a network of more than 600 young people providing support in the form of rides, funding, abortion doula support, and more. They connect with one another to offer informational, emotional, physical, and practical support to other young people seeking abortions. They offer up their own abortion stories in solidarity and as vehicles for change.

As more and more states ban abortion, campus access becomes an ever more crucial part of the abortion access landscape. Many college and university students rely on their campus health centers for medical care—as I did when I was seeking my abortion and assumed I could access it through a large campus health center. Here, too, young people are making their impact by urging administrators to provide medication abortion on campus in states where abortion remains legal, and to put in place frameworks that will support student access to out-of-state care in states where it does not. Providing medication abortion on campus is critical for student care, but also has the knock-on effect of reducing the patient load of clinics that are already overwhelmed and overburdened by people traveling from ban states. In states that do ban abortion, colleges are not without options; they have a responsibility to support student travel to access abortion care through flexible attendance policies, funding for travel, and policies that ensure student confidentiality. University administrators have the power to support the abortion access movement even after *Roe*—and young people are not afraid to hold them accountable for their responsibility to support students and abortion seekers.

Emboldened by this new generation of abortion rights activists, today I speak out about my own abortion freely and without shame. I consider it an honor to work alongside the young people who are leading the movement for abortion justice. They refuse to accept a future without the right to bodily autonomy. They are passionate and they are focused and they deserve our support—we cannot let them do this work alone.

TAMARA MARZOUK (pronounced Tam-uh-ruh Mar-zook) (she/her) is Director of Abortion Access at Advocates for Youth, where she supports a national network of youth activists working to increase abortion access in their communities through practical support, policy advocacy, and storytelling. Tamara is a licensed clinical social worker and public health program developer who has spent her career focusing on the intersection between youth development, mental health, and reproductive justice.

A LETTER TO MY MOTHER
(AND LIKE-MINDED INDIVIDUALS)

MINA ROW

Dear Mom,

I remember going to the first Women's March in 2017—I was only nine. I remember the packed rest stop where women had taken over the men's restroom because there just wasn't enough space. I remember you telling me your friends were knitting pink pussy hats in the back of their car and they would meet us there. I remember the crowds, and the clear backpacks, and the kids who climbed up on top of a stack of plastic pallets with me at the DC mall to start a chant. I remember you telling me that Donald Trump being elected was a threat to my rights to my own body.

But when you're nine, being told that you might lose the right to control your own body doesn't sink in all the way. It took a while for that to really hit me, and still I don't think it has done so completely, at least not yet. I'm only fifteen now, and I only got my period a year and a half ago, so until fairly recently these problems barely felt like they affected me. But now, five years after that march, I hear Rachel Maddow telling me that the Supreme Court has repealed the *Roe v. Wade* ruling that kept millions and millions of people safe, and I'm really scared. (And it's not just women who are at risk here; this is about trans and nonbinary people, too—all people with a uterus.) I'm fortunate enough to live in New York, where there are laws in place that will protect me and others from the dangers of this decision, but I know that isn't the case for the majority of the country.

My friends and I don't often talk about what this decision means for our futures, or at least we don't talk about it as much as we should. But I spend a lot of time thinking about it. Just recently, I was reflecting on how fortunate I am to live in a state where laws are being put into place to protect my body. But then I realized I probably won't live here forever. Even if I stay here as an adult, I will probably leave for college. People ask me all the time if I know where I want to go to college (which, for the record, is absolutely absurd, given that I'm only a freshman). But now the deciding factors might have to change. Will I have to consider if it's safe for me to go to a certain college, given the abortion laws in place? College applications and decisions are a big enough job as it is without me having to think about whether it's safe for me to attend a certain college based on the state it's located in.

Will this be one more factor we have to add to college pro-and-con lists, one that the Gilmore girls never had to worry about? Will we have to spend extra time searching for the abortion laws of every individual state to determine whether or not we should risk my going there? Will I have to ask you, Mom, to take me to a Planned Parenthood in the next state over so that I can keep a child I am not able to care for from being born? What about the people who can't tell their parents at all? What is to come of our young adulthoods? Once, it felt like we could be young and free; now we'll always have to plan for the worst scenarios and take every precaution we can. There is no question that everyone should have safe sex, but that's not always possible and it doesn't always turn out that way—so what happens then?

When I look at my future, this is what it looks like to me these days: If/when I get pregnant, I must have my child, no matter the risk to me or the child, and no matter how it happens. After birthing this child, assuming everything goes smoothly, I then may have a hard time feeding them, thanks to formula and supply shortages. Hopefully the child makes it through infancy, after which I will have to send them to school, where they will be under constant threat of gun violence. If they make it through K–12 schooling, I will then have to pay exorbitant amounts of money to send them to college so they can get a job that will pay them a decent wage and also, maybe, make them happy. Then they will repeat the same process that I did . . . and the cycle continues. I don't want to live like this, and it worries me to look at my future in such pessimistic terms—but that's what the truth feels like right now.

Mom, I'm scared. I'm scared for me, I'm scared for my friends, I'm scared for everyone this ruling affects. I don't know what to do. For now I'm safe, but who knows how long that'll last? And who knows what comes next? Will it be my right to get married? To access contraception? You never even lived in the pre-*Roe* world and now here I am, facing one. How do we convince them our rights matter? What do we do now?

Love,
Mina

MY DAUGHTER'S FIRST PRO-CHOICE PROTEST

ROB GALVIN

It was Tuesday, March 8th, International Women's Day in New York City's own Union Square. The sun was shining bright and there was a slight breeze that brought with it the last remnants of the cold winter chill. I was walking with my daughter; together, we stepped out of the Barnes & Noble store just north of the Square and approached the mass of people already gathered. The crowd in the square was about seventy deep and still growing as we cut through them and advanced towards the stage during setup. My daughter looked up at me, apprehension in her eyes but bravery setting it aside. She stepped forward and picked up a sign that lay on the ground in a pile with a dozen others like it. The bright orange background with large black font read, "Abortion On Demand And Without Apology."

She gripped the sign with both hands and raised the poster board high, letting the stapled cardboard roll rest on her shoulder.

She immediately looked like she belonged in this exact moment where she found herself. This was my daughter's first protest.

Riley is eleven and a fierce feminist who held her placard up as she chanted along with hundreds of others in a sea of orange signs and green bandanas worn to honor the other warriors in solidarity who have fought this battle here at home and abroad. Warriors who won their reproductive freedom in countries like Argentina, Colombia, and Ireland. Countries where women were jailed for "interrupting pregnancies" in clandestine operations and at-home procedures that were life-threatening. Countries where victims of rape, molestation, and incest were forced to carry children to term. Unwanted children coming into the world at gunpoint, essentially. Women in low-income situations who were forced to bear the weight of single motherhood in poverty when some could barely care for themselves, let alone another mouth to feed. Putting their lives on hold while the fathers could freely exit at any moment with little to no consequence. My father was one such individual.

As women find themselves and their right to reproductive justice under constant attack in states across the nation like Texas, Missouri, Florida, Idaho, Kentucky, and Mississippi, each taking women's reproductive rights backward one step at a time, it's clear that this fight needs as much energy as we can muster. I look at my little girl and think of the world I'm leaving her to embrace, the society that is actively working against her right to make educated medical decisions with her doctor and denying her autonomy over her own body. I look at her and think that she deserves more out of this world: a free country that respects women as equal to men, capable of making their own decisions, and recognizes their ownership over their own lives.

I looked at her and then I looked at the mass of people, still growing in number, vibrant and alive in the street, ready to fight for themselves and each other. Standing shoulder to shoulder with other men, women, and more children, all for the same cause and concern. *Roe v. Wade* was under attack, and silence at a time like this felt akin to violence against women.

The speakers began to mobilize and the crowd moved closer together, hundreds of people and hundreds of emotions. Some were happy, some angry, some fed up, and some hopeful. Some cheered and some gritted their teeth, but each and all were there for the fight.

We watched as the speakers, one by one, stepped up to the stage and stood before a backdrop that stated, "We refuse to let the U.S. Supreme Court deny women's humanity and decimate their rights!"

We listened as they invoked emotions of struggle, pain, sadness, and hope. Sunsara Taylor's words brought to life images of women being forced into unwanted pregnancies and subsequently a form of slavery for the rest of their lives. Forced motherhood is female enslavement, nothing short of that.

We felt the sense of desperation that was conjured by the scene of two women holding a giant hanger behind Merle Hoffman as she made her impassioned speech to the crowd beseeching them all to be "Warriors of Light" in this fight for women's right to choose. That sense of desperation that countless American women met in their minds in the decades before *Roe v. Wade* made abortion legal.

We clapped for the words of Gloria Steinem, read by Lori Sokol, Women's eNews Executive Director, comparing the anti-abortion agenda to the Nazi narrative of abortion being a crime against the state as they shut down all family planning clinics. Spotlighting the fact that the right to choose and the right for a woman to have control over her own body are as necessary as the right to free speech, yet are not viewed as fundamental because of patriarchal influence. Pointing out how men being able to absolve themselves of the responsibility of parenthood whenever they see fit after the moment of conception and not having to endure the health risks of undergoing a pregnancy tips the scales in regards to their overall level of indifference. How with the mandating of a vaccine, suddenly every white cis male in the country with wraparound shades and an eight-mile-per-gallon pickup truck is screaming, "My body, my choice." That's the patriarchy hard at work, being as hypocritical as possible.

Then we cheered for Lori Sokol as she expressed the importance of taking this fight from the written word to the streets, where solidarity was seen and felt and the work progressed forward aggressively and in real time. Her words hit differently for me as I looked at my daughter, her first time out in these streets holding her placard up high. This was special: on International Women's Day, at the Rise Up 4 Abortion Rights rally, I was proud to be standing next to her at this place and in this moment.

Originally published as part of the Fe-Man-Ist Voices project at Women's eNews. Created and curated by Amy Ferris and Beth Broday, Fe-Man-Ist Voices is designed to inspire, awaken, enlighten, and encourage men to stand side by side with women in the fight for equality.

ROB GALVIN is a writer and merchant mariner born and raised in Bayonne, New Jersey. The proud father of Tommy and Riley and husband to Kagin Galvin, Rob has been a proud and vocal union member during his career. He is an ally for the LGBTQIA+ community, as well as a proud advocate for women's equality and BLM. Currently based in Dingmans Ferry, PA, he spends his time writing in the mountains when he is not away at sea.

REWRITING THE RULES:
A PHARMACIST'S FIGHT TO
MAKE MEDICATION ABORTION
ACCESSIBLE TO ALL

DR. JESSICA NOUHAVANDI

I've always believed that people should be able to access the health care they need. As a pharmacist, I've seen firsthand the challenges that many people face when trying to find affordable medications. Whether they are uninsured, underinsured, or simply unable to locate a particular medication, the pharmacy world, and more specifically the insurance world, can be next to impossible to understand. And, even if you do understand it, you may still be unable to afford it. It's the problem that my pharmacy, Honeybee Health, was founded to help solve. In 2017, we created an online mail-order pharmacy where people could access generic medications—a place where having insurance, or having good insurance, wasn't a prerequisite for quality and affordable care.

As a female founder of a venture-backed company, the road to funding and running a company like ours hasn't been easy. Female-founded companies have historically received a small share of the available venture capital, and as we worked to grow our business we were no exception; we, too, had to contend with the reality of gender bias in the VC world. Then the spring of 2020 hit, and with the pandemic in full swing, everything became all the more uncertain. Not only were we learning how to navigate a once-in-a-lifetime pandemic personally, we were also faced with the professional challenge of securing funding to support our growth, even as investors were feeling real apprehension in the context of global economic uncertainty. I was feeling discouraged, both as a business owner and as a woman. But I knew our fight to improve health care could not afford to fail. As the only female-led pharmacy in the digital space, I knew there was more work for us to do.

I've always supported abortion as an essential health care service. But until the pandemic, the pharmacy practice was largely removed from abortion care. Medication has long been an available option as a part of abortion care, but because of medically unnecessary and over-politicized regulations, the dispensing of mifepristone (a drug that is used in combination with others to end a pregnancy) was restricted to prescribing clinicians. Prior to COVID-19, pharmacists were not able to dispense the drug—despite the fact that pharmacies have long been some of the most accessible places for people to obtain health care.

But something changed during the pandemic. With the rise of Telehealth practices offering new and innovative ways to keep patients seeking care safe, an opportunity presented itself to revamp how abortion medication was dispensed in this country. For the first time, we in the pharmacy world were given the permission and the tools to say, "This system for dispensing mifepristone doesn't make sense." We were finally empowered to question and be a part of the change our field desperately needed—and at least partly as a result of that, the FDA temporarily suspended the in-person dispensing requirements that had limited dispensing privileges to clinics, hospitals, and medical offices. Because of COVID, the barriers to access became just too great to ignore.

This change opened up a new pathway to providing patients with the care they needed. And at a time in my own life when being a woman felt like it was constantly being used as a point against me, this wasn't just the fight we had before us, it was also the one I needed. So when I was approached in mid-2020 by providers and advocacy groups looking to find a mail-order pharmacy partner to support this work, there was never a hesitation in my mind of "should" we do this; there was only the question of, *How can we get this done?*

Figuring out that "how" turned out to be more straightforward than some might assume: we partnered up with a mifepristone manufacturer, worked out a few important details with providers, restructured a segment of our operational process, and soon enough, we were in business, providing online access to abortion medication. We always understood that there was a possibility that our ability to operate this way would be short-lived, so there were some risks—both financial and legal—involved for us. But our team collectively agreed that the risks were worth taking in order to live out our mission: providing access to affordable health care.

As it turned out, we would have just a few short months, from August through December of 2020, when we would be able to be up and running without interference. We were learning along the way, smoothing out the process of working with providers and finding new ways to improve the experience for providers and patients alike. We were building technology as well, and we felt like we were truly a part of something transformative, as we were not only improving patients' ability to afford necessary medications but also providing whole new avenues to care that had never been available before. We were a part of removing a real access barrier for people, and that made it an exciting and fulfilling time.

Then, in January of 2021, our fears about what might happen to our ability to operate in this way were made a reality when the Supreme Court granted the Trump administration's request to reinstate the FDA's in-person dispensing requirement. It took the wind out of our sails, as we had just gotten this aspect of our practice fully up and running—but we'd always understood this was a possibility. So we shut down mifepristone operations, shipped inventory back to providers, and waited and hoped that the Biden administration would come in and get us back on track.

And in April of 2021 they did just that—once again lifting the in-person dispensing requirement. The administration went a step further still, by requesting that the FDA perform a formal review of the rule, which carried with it the possibility of lifting the restriction permanently. Finally, in December of 2021, the FDA announced that the long standing in-person dispensing requirement had been found to be medically unnecessary, and that medication abortion by mail would remain a permanent option at the federal level. This shift was a huge victory for those of us fighting for patients' rights to access the care they need, and though our pharmacy played a small role in the broader picture of abortion care in the US, I was so proud to be a part of it.

There is no doubt that the overturning of *Roe* represents yet another devastating dive on the roller coaster that has defined reproductive health work over the last fifty years—but I can't help but feel a little bit optimistic nonetheless. Maybe it's because this is the first time the pharmacy practice has been brought into these conversations, so I'm seeing things from the inside more than I ever could before. But what I know now is that the abortion care community is fearless, strategic, and prepared. We have more resources and more knowledge at our disposal than ever before. And this community can move mountains. There are still individual states that place intentional barriers to accessing abortion care, including medication abortion by mail, but there are also twenty-three states where we can now offer our services—and I've never felt more energized about the work still to be done. I know there will be more setbacks and things will be darker for a while, but I also know this: we are not without options.

We've got a long road ahead of us. But it's one I am proud to be walking.

***

DR. JESSICA NOUHAVANDI is the cofounder and lead pharmacist of Honeybee Health, an accredited online pharmacy focused on improving access to affordable generic prescription medications in the US. As a fierce advocate of reproductive rights, she has championed equal access to medication abortion and the integral role of pharmacy in this essential health care service. In 2020, Honeybee Health became the first pharmacy to ship medication abortion pills commercially on behalf of providers. Follow Dr. Jessica on Instagram and Twitter at @drjessicarx.

A BLACK ABORTION
PROVIDER'S PERSPECTIVE
ON POST-ROE AMERICA

BRIA PEACOCK, MD

As a Black woman raised in the South, I have seen how policies affect the ability of marginalized people to make choices about their own bodies and reproduction. Witnessing my older sister become a mother at sixteen years of age and learning that my grandmother birthed my mother at fourteen years of age, I became all too familiar with unintended pregnancies and how the complex intersectionality of racism, sexism, and classism is used to challenge the morality of abortion. Antiabortion activists often take out of context the fact that in the United States, Black women are five times as likely as white women to get an abortion, and they use this fact to push the characterization of abortion as "Black genocide." This claim contributes to the narrative feeding the impending overturning of *Roe v. Wade*.

I've always known this was a false narrative and now, as a Black gynecologist, I see how deeply it's harming our community.

Growing up, I witnessed the consequences of limited access to reproductive choice: perpetuation of poverty, intergenerational "curses," and the resentment experienced by young women who felt forced to have babies and give up their dreams. Watching Black women in my community come to terms with these situations is how I came to my pro-choice values. I wondered what life would be like if these women could decide whether, when, and how to grow their families.

Yet it wasn't until I read up on our nation's history of Black reproductive exploitation that I grew resolute in my perspective. The policing of Black bodies and reproduction dates back centuries, part and parcel of the commodification of Black bodies. The institution of slavery allowed for intrusion into nearly every realm of Black women's lives, including the birthing of babies for profit and labor. Once the importation of enslaved people from Africa was abolished, the reproduction of enslaved people in America was vital to the perpetuation of slavery as a profitable system. For capitalistic gains, white men—doctors and slaveowners alike—increased their interference into the reproductive lives of Black women by means of forced breeding and rape.

In those history books, I saw the women in my community, still struggling with the same oppression generations later, and began to center my life's work on creating community and support for us.

Today, facing the likelihood of a post-*Roe* America, I think about forced births in this population that bears the highest maternal morbidity and mortality in the country. Black women will be disproportionately affected by the lack of abortion access and overrepresented in pregnancy-related deaths. I think about our ancestors each time I support Black women as they give birth or choose not to. I think about the young women of my community whose lives are forever changed by a lack of choice. As a Black female physician,

I aim to ensure that my patients can choose for themselves, knowing that I'm there to support them, not exploit them for anyone's gain.

A few weeks ago, I sat down with a patient who'd decided to terminate her pregnancy. There were many layers that connected us—from our fresh new braids to our love of Southern food. I saw her, and she saw me—multidimensional Black women, unapologetically free in our choices. As I walked her to the procedure room, she asked me why I performed abortions. Caught off guard, I explained this history. I reminded her of her power. There was no need to explain her "why" to anyone; this procedure was her choice, and I supported her fully. She thanked me softly, knowing she was not alone. As I performed her abortion, I thought of that connection and that versatility, recognizing that the very fact of Black abortion providers unapologetically supporting Black women is revolutionary.

In that moment, I felt that unshakeable feeling of pride and joy intertwined with Blackness and its many trials.

That's why accusations that abortion access contributes to the "genocide" of my community shake me to my core. It is not possible for genocide to look like the relief on my patients' faces as I enter the room and put them at ease because I, too, know what it's like to walk through the world as a Black woman.

Forced births and reproductive exploitation of Black bodies are historical facts, and history often repeats itself. When it does, marginalized people usually suffer the most. As I read those history books, I felt that truth. As I walked through life as a Black woman in the South, I felt that truth. As I think about a post-*Roe* America, I feel that truth. But those same history books, that same South, and our future America also contain advocates who understand nonnegotiable reproductive freedoms. We know the plight of Black people who birth babies and have abortions, and we will continue to fight unapologetically for the freedom to safely do both.

BRIA PEACOCK, MD, is an ObGyn resident physician, recently published author, and Georgia native. She is the founder of SIHLE Augusta, an organization that works to positively impact the extreme health disparities experienced by African American women. Dr. Peacock has dedicated her life to serving individuals and communities affected by adolescent pregnancy and high rates of HIV and STIs, and has used her station to be a voice for vulnerable populations wherever necessary—through policy, research, community service, and patient care.

FOR THE PATIENTS

CORDELIA ORBACH

It is early morning, and the winter wind whips off the Hudson River. Despite my decidedly urban location, I am bundled in gear appropriate for summiting a mountain: a hat, gloves, long underwear, hand and foot warmers—winter shifts are long and cold. At this hour, New York City is mostly quiet and calm, but as I approach my destination, the streets quickly begin to echo with voices. I round the corner, and there they are, like a swarm of bees in front of the building, surrounding each newcomer and drowning them in sticky sweet harassment:

> *Hi there, honey. Are you pregnant? We care about you and your baby! Did you know your baby already has a heartbeat? You are a mother today no matter what you do inside. Murdering your baby won't make you not a mother, come and talk to us. You have choices!*

184

Though it is freezing outside, my blood runs hot listening to the (scientifically inaccurate) pleas and co-opting of choice rhetoric that emanates from the people we call "Antis"— anti-abortion activists. I hate hearing it, but I remain focused. I am here for the patients.

As I pass through the crowd, the Antis do not bother me. They know me; they exchange glances with each other and roll their eyes as I walk by.

I don the bright pink smock that reads "CLINIC ESCORT" across my chest and take up my station at the front door. When patients approach, I take a step forward. "Hi, are you looking for the clinic? I can walk with you inside." I project my voice through my mask in an attempt to drown out the other voices and to make the patients feel welcome and safe. I extend my arm to create a space for a patient to find a path to the door.

When patients enter the building, the Antis press their faces into the tinted windows, far closer than the fifteen-foot distance they are supposed to keep from the clinic door. "We know it's scary," they yell into the glass, "but you need to come out and talk to us. Murder is wrong; don't do this." There are no consequences for their actions. They assume everyone who is here is here for an abortion. Some patients will stop and say, "Oh no, I'm just here for birth control" or "I came for STI testing" or "I'm not pregnant, I'm here for a checkup." Some will walk by quickly, earbuds in their ears, tears in their eyes. And some strut past the Antis rolling their eyes and snapping back witty retorts. From under my mask, I try to offer a smile to each person who passes through the door. I am here for the patients.

When there is a lull in appointments, the Antis' commentary turns to me and other escorts. Under their breath, they mock us: "Look what you are doing with your life, murdering innocent children. You could do so much better than this. You don't have to do this, it's evil." I do not engage. Sometimes they stand less than a foot away from me, preaching: "One day, every knee will bow and every tongue will confess that Jesus is Lord." I remain alert, waiting for the next patient to escort safely inside. Scolding and screaming, the Antis launch accusations: "You are a racist, Nazi, baby killer!" I do not dignify them with a response, not even an eye roll. Any tiny reply or response fuels them further. I do not want the space outside to be unsafe, tense, or rowdy. I am not there for them. I am there for the patients.

In early May, after the leaked Supreme Court opinion, local pedestrians—now politically motivated and more aware of the clinic as they pass—walk by in horror with their well-dressed dogs and thank us for being there. "You know what they do in there, right?" the Antis yell. "They murder babies! Are you thanking them for that? You know it's going to be illegal soon?" Some locals stop to argue with the protestors. Quickly exasperated, they turn to us and ask us how we handle it. They cannot believe this is happening in New York City—their city. But it is. This is not a problem reserved for red states. Anti-abortion protestors are not grim reapers hiding in darkness; they are young people with iPhones and old folks with rosaries and Bible verses. They look just like us, and they are even more motivated in the wake of *Dobbs*.

My being there, outside the clinic, isn't a political statement, a well-crafted argument, or a chant screamed out at a rally. I am there to stand firmly for what I believe: all people capable of pregnancy have a right to safe and legal reproductive care. I am there for the patients.

At the clinic, protestors have recently become bolder, louder, more physical. They knock on the windows of cars with partners, friends, or parents waiting outside. They walk up to the door in front of the police. They cheer when patients they harass begin to cry—proof, in their eyes, that God has moved the person not to go through with the procedure.

With increased anti-abortion presence comes increased counter-protestor presence—liberal folks who sing and chant in favor of bodily autonomy. As a result, more police now patrol outside the clinic, drinking coffee and watching from a distance. Out of curiosity, after a shift one day, I asked an officer if he knew about the laws that protect clinic access. He replied that he would look into it; he didn't think any such statutes existed. (In fact, New York City clinics are protected by three clinic access laws: one federal, one state, and one specifically for New York City.)

Witnessing protestors break rule after rule can make shifts all the more grueling. A part of me wants nothing more than to scream at them, "STAND BACK, GET AWAY FROM THE DOOR!" But I am not there to enforce the laws. I am not there to yell in the Antis' faces. I am not there to beg them to behave. I am there for the patients.

I was sending out email confirmations for our weekly Saturday shifts when a CNN banner flashed across my screen: "Roe Overturned." I sat in front of my computer, paralyzed. As I went back to writing emails, my inbox began to ping. First one message, then two, then five, then more. All day and into the weekend, email after email came in: *How can I help? When is your next training session? I was an escort in the '90s and want to begin again.*

Despite my grief, I felt energized—in the face of this despair, I persisted in doing what I could to make sure that the patients walking into our clinic would feel safe and cared for. A friend texted me in anger, *I can't wait till one of them needs an abortion and has to deal with it all alone.* My own reaction caught me by surprise: *They wouldn't be alone. An escort would be there to walk them in.* The fundamental right to reproductive health care includes everyone—even the people standing in opposition to me on the sidewalk. Everyone, including those with whom I vehemently disagree, must have autonomy over their body. Standing outside the clinic, I do not judge who people are or what circumstances have brought them here. To me, that does not matter. If they are walking in the door, I am there for them. I am there for the patients.

One morning, a new escort asked me what to say to people on their way out of the clinic, after their appointments. "Have a good day" feels tone deaf, but saying nothing feels wrong. I always say, "Take care"—it's the only thing that feels right. After *Roe* fell, I kept this sentiment with me. The beauty of this phrase is that care can come in different hues: protesting, crying, escorting, laughing, donating, and voting. During training, we tell new escorts to step inside, drink some water, and take a break when being outside feels too intense. Taking care of ourselves is all we can do and what we must do. We have to take care of ourselves and each other. We have to be there for the patients.

CORDELIA ORBACH is a clinic escort in New York City. A graduate of Bowdoin College with a degree in gender, sexuality, and women's studies, she is deeply committed to ensuring access to reproductive care for all who seek it.

"NO AMOUNT OF PREPARATION COULD HAVE MINIMIZED THE DEVASTATION"

A Q&A WITH MARGARET CHAPMAN POMPONIO, WV FREE

Margaret Chapman Pomponio has more than two decades of reproductive rights work under her belt, but even she wasn't fully prepared for the toll the loss of Roe *would inflict. The longtime leader of WV FREE—an organization that builds stronger West Virginia communities through advocacy and education on reproductive health, rights, and justice—and her team have been working nonstop since the SCOTUS ruling, pushing back on statewide efforts to ban abortion while continuing their essential work training health care workers, direct service providers, and educators in how to deal with unintended pregnancies. It's been grueling— but she remains optimistic about what the future of reproductive freedom holds.*

—EH

EH: WV FREE is the state of West Virginia's leading reproductive health, rights and justice organization and you've been its CEO for twenty years. What brought you to your work in the field?

MARGARET CHAPMAN POMPONIO: I grew up in the '80s in Ravenswood, West Virginia, a small town along the Ohio River once known for its glassmaking. There was an international aluminum plant there, and that meant my family had friends from all over the country and the world. There were also wide income disparities, and I grew up knowing it was unfair that some had so little while others had so much. I think a combination of these things fueled my curiosity, compassion and respect for differences.

My teen years were pretty turbulent. In high school I was in a physically and emotionally abusive relationship with a guy much older than me. I had friends who'd had abortions, and I offered my support as they navigated getting care. By the time graduation rolled around, I was seventeen and ready to get far away from West Virginia. I went to undergrad in the heart of the Rocky Mountains, and through a service-learning project for a sociology class, I worked on a group project to hold Gunnison, Colorado's first pro-choice march and rally. I helped more friends who needed abortions, and that meant traveling for hours over icy mountain passes to get to the closest clinic. Gunnison had a crisis pregnancy center, but no abortion care. It struck me as outrageous, and it fueled my activism.

After attending graduate school in the Pacific Northwest, I eventually ended up back in West Virginia for what I thought would be a temporary stint. WV FREE needed a lobbyist to advocate for reproductive rights, and I jumped in. It turned out that all of my prior experiences were leading me to WV FREE, which I know now to be my life's work. Before the end of that first year, I was named Executive Director of FREE, and I pledged to further the reach and impact of the organization.

EH: I suspect most people don't know much about life in West Virginia. What can you tell us about the realities the residents of your state face?

MCP: West Virginia is the only state located entirely within the Appalachian Mountains. The terrain is rugged, the poverty is high, and the internet connectivity is low, making our population isolated.

We are ground zero for the opioid epidemic and have the highest overdose rate in the nation. One of many consequences of that epidemic are burgeoning HIV hotspots due to IV drug use. You see evidence of this in nearly every corner of Charleston as well as up and down the hollows around the state. It's ravaging our people.

When I returned to West Virginia in the early 2000s, I found a state with strong labor unions, a constitution with more protections than the federal one with regard to abortion rights, comprehensive sexual education, Medicaid funding for abortion, no death penalty, and a proud history of seceding from the racist South during the civil war. This made me balk at the stereotypes of West Virginia that I had become acquainted with during my travels.

Over the years I've realized it's more complex than this. We didn't learn about slavery in our own state through the public education system growing up, or of the rich labor history of the mine wars and Mother Jones. Our history was whitewashed, and I continue to work to learn and unlearn in order to better understand an ever-changing situation regarding race, class, and gender.

EH: Given what you saw as a fairly robust reproductive health context when you returned to West Virginia, what led to the need for an organization like WV FREE?

MCP: The ideology of conservative evangelical churches within our state has permeated our politics. When I started with WV FREE, we were a deep blue state, but even with Dems in charge of the legislature and governor's mansion, anti-abortion bills flooded every legislative session. At that point they were generally stigmatizing bills that didn't really do much to hamper access. A very vocal and pushy minority was driving the politics of abortion. Democrats used the issue to turn out the conservative Democratic base, which created apathy in progressives; they felt the party platform and progressive issues were being sidelined. We became a red state in 2014. It was a painful transition with real consequences. We were fighting like hell.

By 2016, Trump had taken hold. In 2018, West Virginia lost our Medicaid coverage of abortion through a narrowly passed constitutional amendment that said, "Nothing in this constitution secures or protects the right to abortion or requires the funding of it." That passed by little more than three points. If we'd had more investment to connect with voters all over the state, I'm 100 percent convinced we'd have won, as just happened in Kansas. The closeness of our vote shows that we are nowhere near a rock-solid "pro-life" state.

All in all, I know West Virginians are compassionate people. I know this through our voter engagement, polling, and my own personal interactions all over the state. If you ask someone if they're pro-life, they'll say yes, but in the very next breath, they'll tell you the government shouldn't be in charge of reproductive health decisions. We are complex people.

EH: What does WV FREE's work around reproductive health look like on a daily basis? What are your priorities?

MCP: We consider ourselves an education and advocacy non-profit that fights for reproductive health, rights, and justice. Our vision centers on respect for people's lives with the belief that access to reproductive health care and education is a fundamental human right, essential for equity, health, and dignity. Though we don't label ourselves as a reproductive justice (RJ) organization per se (WV FREE's staff is led by a white person and RJ organizations center the leadership of Black women), we are wholly committed to the holistic approach to reproductive rights that RJ calls for. We work for racial justice and LGBTQ rights through partnerships, alliance building, and policy advocacy. Working in coalition is core to who we are and all that we do.

WV FREE trains health care and direct service providers and educators on how to make referrals for unintended pregnancy—either to adoption services or to abortion care. We call them "comprehensive pregnancy options" trainings. This is not just good for an individual who needs care; it creates cultural change, one training at a time. People may start out personally opposed to abortion but end up being able to refer clients or patients to an abortion provider. That's pro-choice and that's progress. And in the post-*Roe* reality, this program will be more important than ever.

Until recently, WV FREE has also offered a strong sex ed training program. But funding has dried up for that and we've had to step away from it. It's sad for our children and our educators, especially at a time when they've lost their reproductive rights. We should be redoubling our commitment to sex ed and contraception like never before.

We also do a lot of targeted voter outreach and mobilization, working in partnership with other progressive groups, and we've been able to get some really great proactive policy passed. We were one of the first states to pass contraceptive equity legislation, a Pregnant Workers' Fairness Act, expanded Medicaid, pharmacy accessible birth control, and much more. We spend most of our time in the public policy arena fighting back scores and scores of bad bills, unfortunately.

EH: June 24, 2022 is a day many of us will remember for the rest of our lives. How has your work changed since the Supreme Court officially overturned *Roe*?

MCP: No amount of preparation could have minimized the devastation. West Virginia doesn't have a trigger ban, but we do have an old 19th-century criminal statute that went back into effect; it imposes a minimum three years in prison for committing the crime of abortion. So our state's only remaining abortion clinic had to cancel terminations immediately or ostensibly risk jail time for patients and providers alike.

The statute was quickly challenged in Circuit Court, however, and an injunction was granted. Abortions were legal again, but the far right went right to work to push forward a total ban on abortion in a special legislative session called by the governor. We were outraged. We mobilized the troops, and the public absolutely flooded the capitol. Remarkably, legislators pushing the ban were surprised by the intense and steady public outcry. We vastly outnumbered anti-abortion advocates throughout the session, and the noise we made could be heard throughout the marble corridors. We knew this could be our last stand for abortion rights for a very long time, and we weren't going down without a hell of a fight.

We networked with doctors, child health advocates, and numerous stakeholder groups to get significant changes to the bill. By the end of it, the conservatives were fighting among themselves. They couldn't settle on a bill, and they adjourned with nothing to show for it but a wide swath of angry, mobilized West Virginia voters. We haven't stopped organizing, and the public is still fired up. We intend to channel the outrage to the next session of the legislature, all the way to the ballot box.

That is some of what we've been doing most recently. At the same time, because WV FREE is uniquely positioned to work with leaders in both the health care and the legal fields, we've also been connecting OB/GYNs and family medicine doctors to our attorney—who is offering free legal interpretations of how abortion criminalization affects doctors' ability to offer care and helping them understand liability risks. There's confusion over how miscarriages and ectopic pregnancies should be handled. We've also been coordinating resources to abortion funds, and ramping up our trainings on self-managed abortion. We are working with our partners to educate the press and the public on the new landscape. It's been nonstop, round-the-clock.

EH: What worries you most about the post-*Roe* era?

MCP: I'm worried about outrage turning into apathy. We have so much to be indignant about right now—the attacks on voting rights, on our very democracy, abortion, and so on. It appears SCOTUS is poised to do huge rollbacks on our rights across the board. The fact is, our country is on a dangerous path and we need people to be on high alert. It's not enough to just vote—we have to broaden the work and get out of our bubbles. We have to organize.

I'm also worried about the purity tests on the left. I think apathy and outrage are tied to that. There's a growing tendency to write people off if they aren't exactly as we'd like them to be, philosophically or politically. There's not a lot of forgiveness, or even inquisitiveness, and that doesn't give people much space to grow. I love Loretta Ross and Toni

Bonds's critiques of cancel culture, and their push for us to call each other in versus calling each other out. We need more of that. There's too much cannibalism in our justice movements and it stifles progress and our ability to connect with everyday folks.

EH: Are there aspects of your work that make you feel optimistic, despite the current context?

MCP: Young people are fired up like never before, and that's the silver lining of this entire disaster around the erosion of abortion rights. When *Roe* fell, they flooded the streets around the state in protest. I saw them take the mics and pledge to mobilize. We've got to channel that into leadership and engagement across movements for social justice.

EH: As you look at the reproductive health landscape before us, are there particular challenges and opportunities you see for organizations like yours in the coming years?

MCP: Philanthropy makes justice work happen, and we're all so deeply grateful. But the nature of it as of now is very "boom and bust." Operating in a scarcity model when there's so much wealth out there is sad and can be quite damaging to the communities that are already hurting the most.

The boom-and-bust model acutely impacts central Appalachian states like West Virginia, where being poor is compounded by race and gender. My hope is that funders can come together to ensure there aren't areas that are under-resourced—both geographically and programmatically. We need to support this work everywhere if we are going to have movements equipped to lead for real social change.

Investments for the general support of organizations working at the state level are going to be critical to our long-term success. We need to fund abortion work, but not just that—we need funders to embrace the importance of supporting intersectional work, understanding that the right to abortion, or even birth control, is basically meaningless if there is limited access to reproductive health care due to institutionalized oppression based on racism, heterosexism, classism, ableism, and so on. We be must intersectional in all that we do. That is where the power and the beauty of this movement comes from. And that is how we win.

***

MARGARET CHAPMAN POMPONIO (she/her) is a seasoned advocate and leader in social justice work who has led WV FREE, a reproductive health, rights, and justice organization, since 2002. She has received national recognition for her work, including a "Woman of Vision" award from the Ms. Foundation for Women. She is active in refugee resettlement efforts, and enjoys travel adventures with her family.

ABUSE, DISCRIMINATION, EXCLUSION: TRANSGENDER MEN EXPLAIN DOMINO EFFECT OF LOSING REPRODUCTIVE CARE POST-*ROE*

ORION RUMMLER

The 19th News

The loss of federal abortion protections has launched America into a new reality: the ability to access abortion depends on where you live. Millions of people have been impacted by this shift, but among the most vulnerable are transgender men and nonbinary and gender-nonconforming people. Without the abortion protections provided under *Roe v. Wade*, this group—already facing discrimination in medical treatment—suddenly is up against barriers that will be insurmountable for many.

"It's very hard for cis people to understand how scary it is to seek health care as a trans person," said Quinn Jackson, a trans primary care doctor in Kansas City, Kansas. "And I think that people who haven't had abortions have no idea how scary it is to seek abortion care, especially in restrictive places. And very, very few people have any understanding of how scary it is to do those at the same time."

The highest concentration of trans people in the United States is in the South, which is also where some of the most stringent abortion restrictions or bans are in place. But while some people who are seeking abortions will go out of state, others—especially Black trans people and other trans people of color—are often left with few or zero options.

They are more likely to struggle with poverty and job discrimination, and many lack the financial resources to cover the procedure and ballooning costs of travel. As of 2015, nearly one-third of respondents to the US Trans Survey, the most in-depth examination of transgender life in the country, were living in poverty—more than twice the rate of the rest of the country.

The prospect of traveling hundreds of miles to another state to get an abortion, and doing it safely—let alone finding a trans-competent abortion provider in a totally new area— is daunting.

Jamison Green, a former president of the World Professional Association for Transgender Health who has written extensively about the lives of trans men, is worried that *Roe* being overturned coincides with rising violence targeting trans people, as more states introduce and pass anti-trans bills. Many trans men and nonbinary people already have to seek abortions and reproductive health care in clinics that emphasize all their services are meant for women. Patients are under threat of abuse or harassment for not conforming, Green said.

He's especially concerned about trans and queer people of color dealing with "a powder keg waiting to explode" as they seek abortions in a post-*Roe* world—racism, transphobia, homophobia compounding all at once.

"People do get abused in settings where gender is highly policed, and where people can't possibly conform to a gender expectation," he said.

Meera Shah, Chief Medical Officer of Planned Parenthood Hudson Peconic in New York and Medical Director of Whole Women's Health Alliance in South Bend, Indiana, has heard about many poor experiences that her trans and nonbinary patients have had in the past with their doctors.

"A lot of my transmasculine patients tell me that they are having sex in a way that could result in a pregnancy, and aren't offered a pregnancy test, they have to request it, oftentimes," she said. Other patients have told her that past providers didn't talk with them about their risk for HIV or about the preventive drug PrEP.

Rodrigo Heng-Lehtinen, Executive Director of the National Center for Transgender Equality, worries that clinics billing their care as "women-only" are already keeping trans people from accessing abortions. When a procedure is only referred to as something for women it makes it tougher to access, he said, whether that comes from just trying to find a welcoming facility, discrimination from a health care provider, or the insurance company turning down coverage.

Heng-Lehtinen pointed to the fact that so few trans people regularly get pap smears to screen for cervical cancer on time as one example: only 27 percent of trans respondents to the 2015 US Trans Survey had done so within that previous year.

"Pap smears are thankfully not stigmatized like an abortion is, but it shows that when a procedure gets coded as being for only one gender and that's just wrong, that actually doesn't describe the people who get that service, then it ends up influencing who actually gets it," he said.

A lack of access, either through state laws or these barriers trans people face within the health care system, could have dire consequences. Several trans men told *The 19th* that the idea of being pregnant earlier in life would have caused them to consider suicide or would have greatly harmed their mental health. While some trans men choose to get pregnant when starting a family, for others the psychological conflict stemming from being pregnant when living as a man would be nothing short of unbearable.

Kylar Broadus, founder of the Trans People of Color Coalition, said that fear is personal for many trans men, especially as they encounter high rates of rape and sexual assault.

"If I had had to carry a child, my spirit would have been broken. And I would have considered killing myself. And that was always one of my fears as a young person," he said.

The 2015 US Trans Survey found that nonbinary people and trans men report being sexually assaulted at a higher rate than other LGBTQ+ people. Fifty-one percent of trans men and 55 percent of nonbinary people out of over 27,000 respondents said they had been assaulted in their lifetime.

The assault that many trans men face, alongside discrimination and harassment that aims to invalidate their identities, has not faded over the years, said Broadus.

"It's just become a pure rape culture out there for trans men in particular," he said. "This law will be horrific."

Camden Hargrove's first concern is how *Roe* being overturned will affect his daughters. But Hargrove, the national organizing manager at the National Black Justice coalition, is also afraid about what will happen to trans men who are assaulted and can't access abortion services.

"I'm absolutely terrified about that for all of my trans brothers, and trans people in general," he said.

The overturning of *Roe v. Wade* could also put other medical services at risk, multiple experts told *The 19th*. Whether trans patients are seeking an abortion or primary care, local independent abortion clinics or Planned Parenthood are often the only place—especially outside major cities—to find gender-affirming care.

"For many of us, Planned Parenthood clinics have been lifesavers because their staff have been trained on trans care and nonbinary care," said Victoria Kirby York, deputy executive director of the National Black Justice Coalition.

Losing gender-affirming care if clinics are forced to close would have an immediate impact, Shah said, noting that Planned Parenthood plans to keep health centers open for services unrelated to abortion care in restrictive states.

"A lot of abortion providers have become a place where trans and nonbinary patients can access hormones, and if those centers are forced to shut down, then those patients could potentially lose a safe, non-judgmental, culturally sensitive place to receive health care," she said.

Jackson is particularly worried about independent clinics, especially because some data suggests that they—rather than larger networks like Planned Parenthood—have provided the majority of abortions in the country.

"Those clinics are also at a really high risk of closing," he said.

The health care challenges faced by trans people—especially in reproductive care—are even more difficult for those who are Black, experts told *The 19th*. Many are mistreated, improperly diagnosed, or just not listened to in doctor's offices, said Hargrove. Others are afraid to go to the doctor after dealing with being misgendered and invasive questions.

"I can foresee so many issues that will really impact trans people, trans men," said Hargrove. "It's gonna be a hard road. It'll be a long fight, but we're here for it."

Non-Hispanic Black women are at least three times as likely as non-Hispanic white women to die from pregnancy-related causes, per the Centers for Disease Control and Prevention. Black women's pain and medical concerns are often outright dismissed by doctors, including during pregnancy, as experts say racism, bias, and less access to quality care all contribute to that high maternal mortality rate.

While the same level of data collection for Black trans men and nonbinary or gender-nonconforming people doesn't exist, experts and advocates believe the same health care disparities are disproportionately harming them—meaning that they will likely be exposed to even more barriers to find adequate care than other trans people.

Grayson Schultz, based in Ohio, works as a care coordinator for LGBTQ+ people across the country seeking health care.

Now that *Roe* is overturned, Schultz expects Black and Indigenous trans people, and other trans people of color, will be the most harmed as they seek to access reproductive and gender-affirming care.

"If you are trans and become pregnant and you need to access abortion services in the South, your options are really, really limited right now," he said.

This story was originally published by The 19th and is reprinted with their permission.

ORION RUMMLER is a reporter on *The 19th*'s breaking news team. He previously anchored live news coverage of events including the January 6 Capitol attack, the coronavirus pandemic, and the 2020 election at Axios. He also researched "Axios on HBO" stories on former President Donald Trump and expanded the outlet's LGBTQ+ coverage.

MY STORY

AMY FERRIS

What so many folks don't understand is that abortion, for what it's worth, is rarely a casual walk in the park; for some of us—for me—it can certainly be categorized as a deeply, profoundly difficult choice. My abortion didn't leave me feeling gaga and giddy and hey, let's celebrate and dance (as people who demonize abortion would have you think). It left me feeling unbearably sad and emotionally fragile, and the residue, in every way, lasted for what felt like a lifetime.

I still wouldn't change a thing.

In my case, an abortion came after giving myself away to a boy who didn't want me or love me and the chances of him wanting or loving me because I was pregnant were slim to none.

(Lesson learned: you cannot get a person to love you who does not want to love you, and a baby is not a carrot—you cannot dangle it.)

I had an abortion when I was very young. I was not cautious, the boy was not cautious—we did not use birth control—and when I missed my period, I most certainly was not prepared in any way to carry a child, to have a child, to support a child, or, most importantly: to love a child. I couldn't love myself; I was a wild, rebellious child who had dropped out of school and left home and had no fucking idea, no clue whatsoever, who she was in the world.

None. Zero. Zip.

The scars from that time in my life are with me still. Not just the physical scars but the emotional and psychological ones, too. Painful scars. I had no idea, none, that my body was a treasure tower, and that how I treated it was vitally important. I had no idea that how I treated my body, that what—and who—I allowed into my body, was of utmost importance. I had no respect for my own body and my body, in turn, repaid that favor.

I know better now.

A few years after that first abortion and after much promiscuous sex, I was diagnosed with both PID (pelvic inflammatory disease) and endometriosis, a horrific combination in the pain department. I spent twelve days in Lenox Hill hospital to treat those diseases—the surgery and post-surgery were both awful.

A few years later, I was told by the same doctor who had performed the surgery that I could never have children. I was also told that the abortion I'd had was *not* the cause of that profoundly sad announcement. It was a combination of many, many choices, some unsavory, some uneducated, some naive. A confluence of some very bad decisions—i.e., men, and not loving myself, not respecting my own life.

It was a wake-up call.

Our.

Bodies.

Our hearts, our souls, our minds, our muscles, our beings: *our* lives.

It is our full-on responsibility to love our bodies, to treat our bodies with deep respect and profound compassion; to value our bodies, to not take them for granted; and, more importantly and most importantly, to not allow anyone, not one soul, to take ownership over our bodies. To not allow anyone to take ownership over our feelings, our choices, and, yes, our mistakes—the ones we make and the ones we sleep with.

To deprive us of any of that—those feelings, those experiences, those opportunities to fall in love with our own lives, to understand our worth and our value, to take back what was stolen from us as children as young women as women—is wholly disgraceful.

To take those choices from us—the very choices that build our souls and our characters, the very choices that come to define who we are and how we love, the very choices that make us better women, better humans—to rob us of that agency? How very inhumane.

All of who I am, every bit of me, comes directly from all the choices—the good the bad the unsavory the tragic the joyous—I have made. And no, no . . . you are not going to take any of that from me, or from any of the women I love and hold dear.

In the wake of recent events, the loss of *Roe*, I find myself thinking about what would have happened to me had I not been able to access an abortion. What would have happened to my life? What would have happened to that young, wild, rebellious girl, that delightfully curious girl, who had secret dreams—big, untamed dreams—of using her voice to one day help change the world?

I can tell you with absolute certainty that she would not have survived if she hadn't had her freedom—the freedom to live her life, the freedom to become. She—I—would not be here today. And I would wager that many women, on reflection, would say very much the same thing.

Roe didn't save my life, in literal terms. But it afforded me the glorious, messy, bold, and, yes, audacious life I've been able to live because of it.

For that privilege, I wouldn't change a thing.

AMY FERRIS is an author, a writer, a screenwriter, an editor, and a playwright. She serves on the Advisory Board of the Women's Media Center, cofounded the Milford Readers & Writers Festival, and is on Faculty of the Kauai Writers Conference. Amy was named one of *Women's eNews*'s "21 Leaders for the 21st Century" and recognized for being one of "12 Women Who Changed the World" in 2022 by NextTribe. She is also the director of the Story Summit Writer's School. Her fervent wish is for all women to awaken to their greatness.

PUSHING BACK ON
THE POLITICS OF HYPOCRISY

SONALI KOLHATKAR

The Supreme Court's recent decision to overturn *Roe v. Wade* was predictable even as it was shocking. Right-wing forces have spent years working painstakingly on multiple fronts in plain sight to ensure that the right to an abortion would no longer be guaranteed, and they have won. Two of the three Supreme Court Justices, Brett Kavanaugh and Neil Gorsuch, who were appointed by former President Donald Trump, stand accused of lying about their positions on abortion. A third, Justice Clarence Thomas, invited challenges to same-sex marriage and the right to contraception as part of his undoing of *Roe*, hinting at the right wing's future targets.

Contrary to the idea that men have foisted the abortion ban on women, the ban is in fact a patriarchal attack by conservatives—men *and* women—against the rest of us.

So many forces had to align in order to ensure that women (and anybody with a uterus) will be forced into taking a pregnancy to term that one wonders how—in light of other catastrophic emergencies like climate change and gun violence—could abortions be considered dangerous enough to ban. Are we not toying with death enough in the United States that we have to add to the ongoing tally of preventable deaths, the casualties that will result from botched abortions?

The answer may lie with a general attitude that forms the basis of most right-wing attacks: that the denial of rights will only affect someone else. Conservatives have perfected the art of outsourcing empathy. When others suffer, they must surely deserve it. And, when conservatives are personally impacted, they are the exception to the rule.

Stories abound of conservative women who picket abortion clinics quietly coming in through the back door to get their own abortions taken care of. One abortion provider told the *Daily Beast*, "All of us who do abortions see patients quite regularly who tell us, 'I'm not pro-choice, but I just can't continue this pregnancy.'" She added, "These are not people who turn anti-choice after having an abortion, but who simply access this essential service when they need it in spite of their personal beliefs about abortion in general."

The results of a survey of women who had abortions, commissioned by an anti-abortion Christian fundamentalist group called Care Net, are instructive. Seventy percent of the 1,038 women surveyed claimed a belief in Christianity and 43 percent attended church monthly. Furthermore, nearly two-thirds of them worried that fellow churchgoers would negatively judge a single woman for being pregnant and only 7 percent openly discussed their decision to get an abortion.

In other words, those claiming to be against abortion for everyone else seek it out quietly when they need one. It's a classic case of "do as I say, not as I do."

This sort of logic of selfishness informs most conservative attacks on the needs of human beings and is based on an enduring belief that they are the exception to every rule.

Take gun violence. Those supporting the complete and easy availability of weapons of mass violence have no problem abiding by safety laws that protect the powerful. Armed members of the public are allowed nowhere near Supreme Court justices, members of Congress, or current and former presidents. Guns are also prohibited at National Rifle Association conventions when current or former presidents speak. The rationale is that when certain people's safety is at stake, it's okay to prohibit guns. The rest of us—even children and the elderly—have to risk living among armed and dangerous people.

Take government welfare programs. Conservatives love to rail against aid to vulnerable populations. Republican lawmakers have made it their mission to slash what they have dubbed as "entitlement" programs for years. But it's *their* voters who often rely most heavily on food stamps and other benefits. In fact, white Americans, who are overrepresented among conservatives, tend to support welfare programs, until they discover those programs might also help people of color.*

Take voting rights. Conservatives and Republicans want to make it harder for people to vote in a nation that already struggles with voter turnout. This effort, intended to ensure minority rule, is premised on a false claim that millions of people vote for Democrats illegally. But in fact, according to a November 2021 article published by The Bulwark, most of the very small handful of people caught illegally voting have turned out to be Republicans.

Circling back to abortion, it's a fair bet that if anti-abortionists had a way to ensure their own personal access to abortion when they needed it, and a ban for everyone else, they might choose such a logical leap.

---

* Chauncey DeVega, "White Americans support welfare programs—but only for themselves, says new research," *Salon*, August 1, 2018, https://www.salon.com/2018/08/01/white-americans-support-welfare-programs-but-only-for-themselves-says-new-research

There was a time when abortion was seen as the first resort of birth control for sex-crazed teenagers. Such visions fueled a fundamentalist Christian worldview of rampant promiscuity among the youthful heathen masses. But today's typical patient needing an abortion is a low-income woman in her late twenties who has already had one child and cannot afford another one.

In fact, abortions are so common that nearly a quarter of all people capable of pregnancy will have one in their lifetimes by age forty-five. That percentage may be even higher considering that researchers find people severely underreport their abortions.

Part of the problem is that until recently there has been little narrative work done by organizations supporting the right to an abortion to destigmatize the procedure. Now more and more people are coming forward to tell their stories, most of which are mundane tales about forgetting to take contraception or finding that their birth control method failed.

Hollywood has been particularly egregious in helping to cloak abortion access in a pall of shame. Recall the wildly successful 2007 film *Juno* starring Elliot Page as a pregnant teen who decides against getting an abortion and carries an unwanted pregnancy to term. The film was typical of how Hollywood treated characters struggling with unwanted pregnancies. Screenwriter Diablo Cody concedes that she wouldn't write such a plot in today's political environment, saying, "In a way I feel like I had a responsibility to maybe be more explicitly pro-choice, and I wasn't."

Cody is not alone. So-called liberals in Hollywood have written so many anti-abortion tropes into their plot lines that some years ago activist Fatima Goss Graves pleaded with women writers at a conference to begin normalizing abortions on screen. Her exhortation appears to have worked, and works of fiction are finally treating abortion as the mundane and shame-free health procedure that it is. But it's too little, too late, and years of invisibility and shame paved the road to *Roe* being overturned.

There will come a time when anti-abortion conservatives finding themselves in need of abortion services will have nowhere to turn to, becoming the victims of their own wild success. The realization that abortions are part of necessary health care that even *they* need will also be too little, too late.

This article was produced by Economy for All, a project of the Independent Media Institute.

SONALI KOLHATKAR is the founder, host, and executive producer of *Rising Up With Sonali*, a television and radio show that airs on Free Speech TV and Pacifica stations. She is a writing fellow for the Economy for All project at the Independent Media Institute.

IS VIOLENCE THE LAST GASP OF THE PATRIARCHY?

GLORIA FELDT

During my half-century of working for women's equality, I've often said the violent reaction to women's progress was simply the last gasp of the patriarchy. Then, bingo, it rears its head again, like Groundhog Day. Cue replays of *The Handmaid's Tale*.

On January 6, 2021, we watched in horror as a vicious attack on the Capitol threatened to turn America into the authoritarian country my grandparents came here to escape. A year later, as the media replayed clips from January 6, I wondered why no one was connecting the dots between this insurrection, what was then the probable demise of *Roe v. Wade*, which represents women's right to reproductive self-determination (and has since been overturned), and lack of action to ratify the Equal Rights Amendment—all of which fuel the pervasive gender gap in power, pay, and leadership roles.

Photos of members of Congress hiding under the benches and the feral clawing at the Capitol windows by a howling mob that was 86 percent male and 93 percent white took me back to my years leading Planned Parenthood at the peak of attacks, up to and including murders, on reproductive health providers.

When the targets of such vitriol and violence were "just" women, law enforcement was slow to act if at all. Media reported with false equivalence, akin to Trump's "good people on both sides" assessment of the 2017 white supremacist, anti-Semitic mob in Charlottesville. The brave women and men who served family planning and abortion patients despite this antipathy took on a bunker mentality. The burden was placed on Planned Parenthood, and our patients, to protect ourselves; the organization spent vast sums of money beefing up security. I once had to get the mayor to intervene when, rather than protecting us, our police chief told us to "close our clinics" if we heard an incursion was planned.

HOW DID THIS HAPPEN?

In analyzing the events of January 6, 2021, equality advocate Jackson Katz correctly acknowledges "the insurrection was an overt and violent assertion of white male centrality and entitlement." A look back at the history of reproductive rights and justice clarifies that racism and sexism are joined at the heart of women's struggle to achieve bodily autonomy.

White men have always had a legal and moral right to their own lives, but neither the court of law or the court of public opinion has declared unequivocally that women's rights are human rights and human rights are women's rights after all.

The purposefulness of pregnancy among most women in America is evidence of many victories: Contraception was legalized by the US Supreme Court in *Griswold v. Connecticut* in 1965, and pre-viability abortion was legalized by *Roe v. Wade* in 1973. Yet these victories carried the seeds of their own demise, because the decisions are not grounded in an assertion of the moral and legal agency of women; instead, they're based on an assumed right to privacy.

Paradoxically, the personal freedom to make childbearing decisions privately had to be won through the political process. Author Jane Smiley rightly observed that pregnancy is the most public of conditions, and the state of a woman's uterus is the most public of political battlegrounds.

While I would like to think that the violence we witnessed on January 6 signaled (again) the last gasps of the patriarchy, my time fighting for reproductive rights has shown me otherwise. In many states, it has become more difficult for people to participate in the democratic process—by design. Knowing this, women cannot sit by and hope that any of our hard-won rights will stand the test of time. We must be deliberate, intentional, and persistent to end the cycle of tying women's legal, moral, and bodily autonomy to the whims of a court or politics. First and foremost we must always be leading with a vision of full equality for all women, intersectionally. That requires a powerful policy agenda backed up by smart organizing from the grassroots to the grass tops, much as was implemented to defeat the recent Kansas ballot initiative intended to outlaw abortion.

We can never, ever let up, because in a democracy victories won can be snatched away without constant vigilance. Whether we like it or not, the future is in our hands.

WHAT DO WE DO ABOUT THIS?

Because of my long view of history, coming from a lifetime on the forefront of the women's movement, people have frequently asked me this exact question, often from a place of fear rather than power. That must change.

Here's the formula:

Power Up the Message.

Don't be shy. Consistently deliver the values-based message that reproductive autonomy is inherently tied to women's civil, moral, and human rights to live as equal citizens, to contribute to the economy, and to never again be "barefoot and pregnant." Enlist the media to amplify the message accurately. Leverage well-timed street theater but don't expect that to win what must be won at the ballot box.

Collect Grassroots Power.

Align with diverse organizations whose missions intersect. Build the movement fearlessly. Hold corporations and politicians accountable by visibly rewarding those who tangibly support women's rights and withholding your business and vote from those that don't.

Women Leaders, Use Your Powerful Voice.

You have the power of your positions because others have fought for you to have these rights. Use it. When corporate women leaders spearhead or visibly support initiatives to secure reproductive rights and justice, other business leaders will follow. Move women's rights out of their silo; build into companies' culture and policies the assumption that women's rights are like other civil rights. This also gives men a much-needed way to fight for the cause and benefit from it.

Keep the Pressure On.

Elected leaders must move urgently to pass federal and state laws that guarantee women's civil and human rights, including the big three—the Equal Rights Amendment, the Paycheck Fairness Act, and the Freedom of Choice Act—along with voting rights. Contact your local and national leaders and be relentless in expressing your views and supporting those whose votes deserve yours in return.

Do not be deterred or discouraged by threats or displays of violence. Stay focused on our goal. We have the power to keep the dystopian world of *The Handmaid's Tale* at bay, to build a world where each of us can make our own childbearing decisions, and onward from there to true equality and justice for all.

Originally published by Ms. Magazine *and reprinted by permission of the author.*

GLORIA FELDT is the *New York Times* best-selling author of several books, including *Intentioning: Sex, Power, Pandemics, and How Women Will Take The Lead for (Everyone's) Good* and *No Excuses: 9 Ways Women Can Change How We Think About Power*. She is a sought-after speaker and frequent contributor to major news outlets, and the cofounder and president of Take The Lead, a leading women's leadership nonprofit working to achieve gender parity by 2025.

WE NEED A POST-*ROE* STRATEGY FOR THE LONG HAUL. GLOBAL FEMINISTS OFFER A BLUEPRINT.

YIFAT SUSSKIND

After the initial shock over the Supreme Court's action against abortion rights, we're all grappling with an inevitable, fundamental question: what now?

We now face a future rewritten by this attack on abortion access, a right-wing power grab over our bodies that threatens our safety, rights, and freedom and that was facilitated by a decades-long coordinated anti-choice effort. US reproductive justice activists will need just as much stamina and determination in our defense of our bodily autonomy and freedom.

But we have allies and teachers in this fight—including in feminist movements worldwide.

As we build a long-term strategy for reproductive justice, we must look towards feminist allies around the world who are fighting for reproductive justice and abortion care for all who seek it, despite legal and political obstacles. From movements to decriminalize abortion in Colombia and Mexico to frontline workers providing abortion care despite criminalization, their work illuminates a path towards safe and accessible abortion care that we can build here at home.

El Salvador is one of the twenty-four nations in the world where abortion is illegal in all circumstances. Federal prosecutors visit hospitals and encourage doctors to report any woman suspected of self-inducing abortion. These women face jail sentences of up to forty years, even when they are simply treating a miscarriage, which requires the same medication used for abortion. Frontline feminist organizations like Agrupación Ciudadana por la Despenalización del Aborto El Salvador and Red Salvadoreña de Defensoras de Derechos Humanos are working against criminalization.

Despite the legal risk, about 5,000 abortion procedures are performed on El Salvador's black market every year. One doctor providing abortion care reports, "I've seen fathers bringing their teenage daughters, taken by force, raped by gang leaders, and left pregnant . . . If those of us who are technically trained don't help, women will have to go elsewhere. They will go to people who have no experience or training."

For pregnant people in their first trimester, abortion care doesn't always depend on surgery: it can also depend on access to the medications mifepristone and misoprostal, aka "the abortion pill."

A Canada-based service, Women on Web, ships the abortion pill to people living in countries where abortion is illegal. Until the abortion ban was repealed in May 2021, people living in Ireland either received abortion pills in the mail from services like Women on Web or traveled to England to get abortions, often using a fake English address. People in the US may face similar options: travel to other states, or even to other countries like Mexico or Canada, where the procedure is not banned, or find services that will ship the abortion pill to you, despite the legal risks. In Mexico, a coalition of feminist organizations are working together to create "a cross-border network of support for safe abortion for Texan women" with plans to expand the network to other states.

Doctors, activists, and patients take on the legal risks of abortion because the alternative is desperation and death. In Brazil, where abortion is illegal, it's estimated that every year 250,000 women are hospitalized, and 200 die, from complications from abortion. When abortion was criminalized in Nicaragua, a prominent gynecologist called it "a government death penalty imposed on women." He was right: maternal mortality increased as people died in childbirth from pregnancy complications and pre-existing conditions exacerbated by pregnancy. And they died from desperation: among the pregnant women who died from causes "unrelated" to pregnancy, 63 percent died of suicide.

It's simple: abortion care saves lives.

It saves the lives of people who want to be pregnant but have miscarriages or complications. It saves the lives of parents who cannot take care of one more child. It saves the lives of people who desperately do not want to be pregnant. It saves the lives of people like Rosaura, who died at sixteen in the Dominican Republic because she was denied chemotherapy, life-saving treatment, because she was pregnant. Her mother, Rosa Hernandez, cried, "they let my daughter die."

Medical providers, networks distributing abortion pills, and legal support networks are the frontline defense of our bodily autonomy, but they are not alone: feminist political groups are organizing political pressure to end punitive abortion laws. And these feminist movements are winning: over the last twenty-five years, nearly fifty countries have liberalized their abortion laws.

In Latin America, new and transformative abortion laws were secured by "the green tide": an international feminist movement for bodily autonomy and abortion access that crossed state borders, identified by the green scarves activists wear at demonstrations. The imagery has historic roots in feminist and economic justice movements, including movements against domestic violence, international feminist strikes, and popular resistance to military rule led by the Mothers of the Plaza de Mayo. During COVID-19, millions of women wearing green scarves joined protests demanding abortion care across Latin America under the banner: "Ni Una Menos. Vivas y libres nos queremos." ("Not One Woman Less. We want to be alive and free.") This feminist framing of abortion as a human rights issue drove home the message that abortion is not a discrete issue but part of the spectrum of rights that guarantees the safety and well-being of people across the region.

It worked. New abortion laws in Mexico and Colombia have been transformative. In 2020, MADRE joined a case at the Colombian Constitutional Court, brought by Causa Justa, to legalize abortion access. We won. In February 2022, abortion was legalized in Colombia through the twenty-fourth week of pregnancy, making it one of the most liberal laws in the world. In Mexico, since the 2021 Supreme Court ruling that abortion is not a crime, hospitals are no longer required to report abortions as a criminal activity, saving the futures of poor women, in particular, who depend on public hospitals for abortion treatment and care.

Bodily autonomy is fundamental: it determines our ability to care for ourselves, to care for others, to exercise economic independence, to build a life of pleasure, and to transform political systems. Authoritarians attack bodily autonomy because the social, economic, and political independence of historically marginalized communities is a building block of change. And that independence rests on the ability to control, and care for, our bodies.

In the US, the criminalization of abortion care won't just dictate the health outcomes of pregnant people: this attack will reverberate throughout the LGBTQ community as an attack on the right to privacy, the right to marriage, and the right to non-discrimination, with consequences as far-ranging as undermining our digital privacy to limiting access to condoms and birth control.

The Supreme Court has taken away a constitutional right and a human right. But the court cannot take away the care we show for one another. The court cannot stop us from providing abortion care if we guarantee it for one another. MADRE remains committed to supporting abortion funds and reproductive justice organizations working to guarantee bodily autonomy and accessible abortion care for all pregnant persons, especially Black, Indigenous, people of color, LGBTQ, and disabled communities who face systemic and historic barriers to non-discriminatory health care.

The court cannot stop us from standing shoulder to shoulder with feminists around the world and working towards that promised future where we see ourselves, alive and free.

This article was originally published on CommonDreams.org and is reprinted by permission of the author.

MADRE Executive Director **YIFAT SUSSKIND** partners with women human rights activists from around the world to create programs in their communities that meet urgent needs and create lasting change. A lifelong promoter of human rights, Yifat leads MADRE's combined strategy of community-based partnerships and international human rights advocacy. Under Yifat's leadership, MADRE has enabled thousands of local women's rights activists from around the world to survive and thrive in the wake of war and disasters.

6 WAYS TO FIGHT FOR ABORTION RIGHTS AFTER *ROE*

KATHA POLLITT

In the wake of the Supreme Court's overturning of *Roe v. Wade*, it's tempting to blame the pro-choice movement. Blaming ourselves: isn't that what we progressives, especially women, love to do? Somehow, it's our fault—for being too white/middle-class/respectable, too beholden to the Democratic Party in return for too few crumbs. Always throwing money at unwinnable races, allowing abortion to be stigmatized ("safe, legal, and rare"), maintaining bloated organizations that lumber and creak and resist change. It's all true—I've written that piece many times. But today I'm not so sure any of that would have mattered. The truth is, Donald Trump came to power despite losing the popular vote by almost three million, enabling Mitch McConnell to ruthlessly engineer the current right-wing Catholic anti-abortion Supreme Court majority, and here we are. The crisis of abortion is a crisis of democracy.

Within Alito's majority, none of them care about public opinion, which is majority pro-*Roe*. Nor, apparently, do they seriously consider the many terrible consequences of forcing so many women into unwanted childbirth. (They can always give the baby away, as Amy Coney Barrett suggested helpfully.) They're in their own theocratic bubble, where anything goes if it supports the holy cause—where, for example, Alito can approvingly cite Matthew Hale, a 17th-century British jurist who sentenced two women to execution as witches and wrote an influential treatise permitting men to rape their wives. Superstitious? Misogynistic? They just don't care.

In the face of this disaster, it's tempting to rant and rave. There's been a lot of that, in print and online, and that's fine. We need passion, articulate and splendid passion, to spur us to the work ahead. But this time I'm going to leave the rage and fire to others—take it away, Rebecca Traister! Instead, I want to think out loud here about what that work might be.

First, we need to bolster abortion rights and access wherever possible, and that means winning elections wherever possible. Frances Kissling, the former president of Catholics for Choice, tells me that the pro-choice movement has little to show for its electoral efforts in red states (remember the massive shower of gold for Wendy Davis?) and should shift its focus to shoring up blue states and providing actual services, such as organizing travel from abortion-ban states. I'm with her on strengthening blue states, but I don't agree about abandoning the red ones. Taking back state legislatures and governorships will be the work of many years—and we can probably be smarter about choosing our battles—but whittling away at anti-choice majorities in the red states has to be on our to-do list, or our problems will only grow worse.

Kissling is certainly right, though, that there's work to be done in Blue America. Currently, sixteen states, as well as the District of Columbia, have enshrined legal abortion in their constitutions or statutes; we need all blue and purple states to do so, because the forces that came for abortion in the red states will come hard at them now. My part-time home state of Connecticut is a shining star here. In May of 2022 it passed not only state constitutional protection of abortion but also laws protecting providers, abortion travelers, and those who help them from the legal reach of abortion-ban states. Connecticut now explicitly codifies the right of some non-MD medical workers to perform some abortions and give out abortion pills.

Second, Kissling argues, we need to energize (polite word) the whole medical profession and hold it to account. Many medical schools don't teach the procedure. We need to force them to do so as part of routine gynecological care, because that is what it is. And what about hospitals? The economics of running a stand-alone clinic can be pretty daunting, especially given low reimbursement rates from Medicaid. That is one reason clinics have been closing, even in blue states. Hospitals could take on some of this work, but few do: In 2017, they performed only 3 percent of abortions, and that includes secular, non-Catholic hospitals. Why? Maybe a big donor is anti-choice. Maybe management fears being targeted by anti-abortion activists. There's not a lot of money in an uncomplicated first-trimester abortion, and potentially a lot of *tsuris*. Tough. We need to pressure hospitals to rise to the challenge and give women an uncomplicated, legal service that one in four of them will need during their fertile years. Indeed, not to do so is a kind of malpractice akin to refusing to treat someone for a widespread, easily cured, but potentially fatal condition because it's just too much of a bother.

Third, we need to push the blue states to fund abortion directly: to subsidize clinic and hospital services, raise Medicaid reimbursements, expand Medicaid to include undocumented immigrants, and make grants to abortion funds that help low-income people pay for their procedures. (The New York City Council has led the way here: since 2019, it has granted $250,000 annually to the New York Abortion Access Fund.) What about blue states setting up bus services to bring red-state patients to clinics? Paying for hotel stays for abortion travelers?

Fourth: Donors—i.e., you—need to step up their giving. There are already way too many women who have to travel for their procedures. That is going to be magnified many times over in the twenty-six states poised to ban or greatly restrict abortion once *Roe* is overturned—and those women will be traveling farther as neighboring states pass bans of their own. Now is the time to give generously to travel funds like the Brigid Alliance, which covers the cost of transportation, plus food, lodging, child care—whatever the patient needs. Give to regular funds as well—the more money they have, the more they can fund first-trimester procedures before patients reach the far more expensive second trimester. The National Network of Abortion Funds holds an annual fundraiser (fundathon.nnaf.org). On its home page, you'll find a map of all its member funds, probably including one or more in your region.

Fifth: Use your imagination. Can you host a traveling patient in your spare room, or even on your sofa? If you run an Airbnb, can you volunteer it one or two days a month? Can you drive someone from a banned state to the nearest clinic? Volunteer as a clinic escort? Mind a patient's children while she's having her procedure? Call your local clinic and ask how you can help. Pro tip: If you are feeling short of money to donate, look over your credit card bills. Believe it or not, there are women who are prevented from ending their pregnancy because they can't pay for a babysitter or a bus ride. Fifty dollars could make all the difference. The fees for that streaming service you never use (ahem!) and that Substack you haven't looked at in months could be transformed into a monthly donation to the Frontera Fund, which helps low-income residents of the Rio Grande Valley access abortion, or Just the Pill, which sends affordable abortion pills by mail and is starting a mobile clinic.

Sixth: Do more. If you are reading this, chances are you are already voting, donating, writing your legislators, and so on, like the good citizen you are. So, go further: Demonstrate incessantly, like the feminists of Argentina and Mexico. Walk out of that anti-choice church you still go to for some reason, like Polish feminists did in 2016 when the government threatened to ban abortion. Put up informative stickers, as Irish pro-choicers did back when it was against the law even to give out the phone numbers of UK clinics. Stand with your friends outside your local crisis pregnancy center, aka fake abortion clinic, and politely hand out leaflets telling people what the place really does.

Remember, though: It's not the 1960s. For every kind of activism you want to get involved in, there are groups working on it already. You don't need to start your own secret network to get pregnant women out of Texas—give to Fund Texas Choice, which already does that. Nor need you personally smuggle abortion pills into states with bans. Even in Texas, people can order pills online and, if necessary, have them mailed to a forwarding address in another state. Thousands of women have already gotten pills this way. What would be helpful? Smith College professor Carrie N. Baker, who studies the abortion pill, suggests you spread information about abortion pills and how to get them safely. Go to plancpills.org for details.

Finally, don't let yourself feel pre-defeated. We can win this eventually, but despair will make it harder. Just concentrate on what you can do now: protecting and expanding rights where possible, supporting abortion services, and, above all, getting pro-choice legislators into office at every level. The progressive activist Heather Booth, a founder of the Jane Collective, which provided clandestine abortions in Chicago pre-*Roe*, told me, "I took two big lessons from the civil rights movement, which also seemed an impossible struggle. One is, sometimes you have to stand up to illegitimate authority. The other is, if we organize, we can win. Even in the face of bad decisions and conflict and trouble, we still need to be agents of hope."

Originally published in The Nation *in 2022 and reprinted by permission of the author. The article has been updated to reflect the Supreme Court's decision on Roe v. Wade.*

KATHA POLLITT is a columnist for *The Nation*. Her latest book is *Pro: Reclaiming Abortion Rights*; she is also the author of two books of poetry and several collections of essays. She lives in New York City.

GIRDING OUR LOINS: A SPIRITUAL SURVIVAL GUIDE FOR THE BATTLE AHEAD

CHAPLAIN LIZZIE BERNE DEGEAR, PhD

Isn't it ironic that a term originating in a male, military, biblical context—a phrase to describe preparing for war—is so apt for what we need to do today in this battle for reproductive freedom and women's autonomy? To gird one's loins is to protect the parts of the lower torso vulnerable to attack.

No doubt about it. We must gird our loins for this fight.

My work as a hospital chaplain has brought me to particular kinds of war zones. I've been with people fighting cancer, battling addiction, and facing the death of a child. Sitting with fellow human beings in the midst of something horrible that threatens to overwhelm, I have often doubted I have anything to offer. I know there is nothing to say or do that will make it better or fix the existential threat they face. But I have come to realize there is a way to join them in the crisis and offer a valuable spiritual resource: I can help create space for people to access their own power.

As we find ourselves today in a post-*Roe* America, I recognize it as a kind of war zone. We need our spiritual resources, and I have a sense of how to muster these resources in this critical moment. We can find and access our power. Here I offer a few ways we can do that on the personal and collective front, girding our loins to prepare ourselves for the difficult work that lies ahead.

1. Recognize the lie and gird yourself in joy. The attack on abortion access is built on lies that attack human reasoning. Perhaps you, like me, feel a maddening rage when you see and hear these lies. Perhaps you, like me, have been trying to fight these lies by doing the social-media equivalent of pointing and shouting, "But that's not true!!"

Calling out America on its lies is how American changemakers have often shown the way forward. In Frederick Douglass's 1852 speech "What to the Slave is the Fourth of July?" the brilliant orator and humanitarian spoke his own declaration of independence from the lie of American freedom/slavery. Declaring that "the hypocrisy of the nation must be exposed," he fumed: "At a time like this, scorching irony, not convincing argument, is needed."

Today, we find ourselves at another such time, faced with yet another American lie. And, oh, how I felt scorching irony burn in me as I read Justice Alito's concluding sentence in the Supreme Court's majority opinion: "The Constitution does not prohibit the citizens of each State from regulating or prohibiting abortion. *Roe* [*v. Wade*] and [*Planned Parenthood v.*] *Casey* arrogated that authority. We now overrule those decisions and return that authority to the people and their elected representatives."

Do you know what "the Constitution does not prohibit the citizens of each State from"? It does not prohibit us from having abortions! But Alito's words attack that truth and twist it into a lie with infuriating doublespeak—arguing instead that the Constitution does not prohibit prohibiting abortion. Oh, the irony in Alito's use of the word "arrogate"—a word which means to seize and claim power as yours when it isn't yours—for that is just what the court has done with its decision to overturn *Roe*. The decision aims to seize the power women have over ourselves and give it to systems of government. Stealing people's authority in the name of "returning that authority to the people and their elected representatives" is outright theft built on lies.

Thus this attack on our bodies is bolstered by justifications that are attacks on human reason. Defying logic, these lies are toxic and can cause us mental harm when we fix our focus on them. By infuriating us with their disregard for truth, these manipulations can sap our energy, draining us and leaving us with an overwhelming sense of despair.

To protect against this toxicity, we must declare independence from the lies. How? First, I encourage you to develop your own practice for noting the lies as they come but not engaging them. Recognize the lie and then powerfully dismiss it. Reject it with a full-bodied gesture that refuses to accept the lie. A gesture I use is to push my palms forcefully away from my body, fully extending my arms while saying, "No! That is a lie!" I do this because the lies and attacks are aimed at our bodies and our minds; finding a combination of intentional physical movement and spoken word effectively dispels the power of the lie. I encourage you to get creative and find a gesture unique to you. One wonderful example can be found an hour into the documentary *Knock Down the House*. Before facing her political opponent in a televised debate, Alexandria Ocasio Cortez creates her own body ritual by moving her arms around her and simply saying, "I need to take up space. I need to take up space. I am here."

Second, distinguish between fighting lies and investing in truths; choose to spend your time and your energy on the latter. Once you've rejected the lie in a physical and intentional way, immediately take the opportunity to reconnect with something real and true that gives you deep pleasure. Remember that you are here. Revisit a favorite line of poetry, or relish the laughter of a beloved elder or toddler. Go for a walk with a friend and then turn to your own important work. In short: Feed your relationship to truth by connecting with humanity on a level that goes much deeper than politics or social media. Reject the lies, connect through joy. Think of this two-part exercise as a form of detox and nourishment that will become more and more necessary as these lies and attacks take hold of our society.

2. Develop your agency, secure your boundaries. When the draconian Texas abortion ban became law in September of 2021, I—along with feminists and womanists of every gender—showed up with my friends at my local rally and protest march. I thought long and hard about what I wanted my sign to say. How could I use my unique voice in a way that felt authentic to all of who I am? I settled on this: "This Catholic Chaplain Believes in WOMEN'S AGENCY." I saved extra-large gold lettering for the last two words because I understand at my very core that these recent attacks on abortion access are an attack on women's agency.

Many metaphors can point us to our agency and show us how to connect with it: it's about trusting your gut, listening to your inner truth, living from your core, developing and staying true to your Self. Do you notice that these images of agency bring us to the innermost center of our bodies? Our loins need girding right now not only because they are vulnerable but also because they are symbolic of each person's agency and power. Those who seek to strip our rights are afraid of our power, and they are right to be afraid. Connected to our agency, and to each other, we tap into a deep strength that far outstrips patriarchy and institution. This is why, in this fight for women's autonomy, each of us must connect profoundly with our own agency and act from there. Your agency is yours. Find it. Develop it. Act from it.

As we develop our human agency, we must also learn how to protect the inner core from which it emerges. Our integrity is under attack. Our sovereignty is being challenged. So this is the time, more than ever, to heal our broken boundaries. This way of girding our loins is a deep practice of self-care and self-knowing. Healthy boundaries develop from within, from our sense of wholeness, rather than out of defensiveness or reactive fear.

The work of mending our boundaries is essential preparation in the fight for justice and our human rights. Girding ourselves in this way takes time and intention. We each must do the difficult, intimate, uncomfortable inner work that is uniquely our own. We need to listen to our gut when something doesn't feel right. We must mourn the personal losses (and the global ones too) that we may have prematurely rushed to get over. And can we find the courage to begin healing the intergenerational traumas lodged in our bodies? These efforts may sound complicated or even irrelevant to the cause at hand, but my own life has taught me otherwise. If we skip over this work, we won't have the energy to fight. If we engage this healing work, we will.

3. Ground yourself. In literal, practical ways, find your physical connection to this planet and strengthen that connection. We access our own power most effectively when we tap into our connection with the earth as the source of all life on the planet.

Humans, as distinguished from other animals and plant life, often act in ways that try to deny the earth's power. In doing so, we limit that natural power from coming through us. Don't cut yourself off from this vital, life-giving source. While we declare independence from the web of lies taking hold of society right now, we can acknowledge and tap into the web of life, letting interdependence empower us. Discover that your power is a renewable energy source by staying connected to the earth.

However this crisis is calling you to action—on the legal front, on the health care front; through protest or donation or advocacy; or even if you are just asking yourself, "What can I do in the face of this attack?"—there is a strong urge in many of us right now to fight fire with fire. But before acting from the fuel of your ignited anger or burning sense of injustice, I encourage you to connect with the other elements too—earth, water, and air.

Each day, if you can, stand on ground that isn't cement or floorboards. Be touched by circulating air that hasn't made its way to you through an air conditioner or hair dryer. Witness water that doesn't come through a pipe or a bottle. Let those elements find you, and in some basic way let them take care of you.

4. Collectively, we can gird ourselves with the fabric woven by this movement. Let us not underestimate the strength of the movement for reproductive freedom and women's agency. Threads in this fabric come to us from every Indigenous culture on the planet. Millennia before there were courts or elected representatives, there were women empowering other women who faced pregnancies and choices about their health. These ancestral threads have been taken up by Indigenous women around the world who live and practice and teach them today. We all can listen and learn.

In the US today, the fabric of our ongoing movement is being woven by thousands of women and others who have been devoting their professional lives and their energies, year in and year out, to women's health and agency. All this time, working together in solidarity and mutual care, they have been weaving networks of reproductive health. Organizations including New Mexico–based Indigenous Women Rising (with an abortion fund open to all Indigenous people in the United States and Canada), United States of Women (where you can pledge to become an abortion advocate), Plan C (providing up-to-date information on at-home abortion pill options), and Black-led agencies such as Sister Reach in Tennessee, Sister Song in Georgia, and the Ayifa Center in Texas are weaving these networks. As a person of faith, I find solidarity in organizations such as the Religious Coalition for Reproductive Choice, Catholics for Choice, and the National Council of Jewish Women, and I find inspiration in the memoir of abortionist-of-faith Dr. Willie J. Parker, *Life's Work*.

These networks are strong. They are flexible. We make them even stronger and we increase their ability to move with the times when we lend our energies and resources to this work already being done.

Lastly, we can find our strength by realizing how intertwined we are with the many movements for justice and well-being that call for our attention right now. We can interweave our actions with all those fighting for equity and peace. A lot is broken in this moment. The structures of our society are failing to serve our collective health and well-being. But rather than simply fearing the aftermath that looms in a post-*Roe* America, we can work collectively to build a new loom, together with all those ready to weave the fabric of a strong and healthy society.

LIZZIE BERNE DEGEAR, BCC, PHD is a writer, teacher, chaplain, filmmaker, Bible scholar, and womanist/feminist. In 2017, she cofounded the Feminism & Faith in Union movement. Her award-winning animated short film *(m)adam: Adam's Rib Reframed* and other works can be found on her website, www.LizzieBerneDeGear.com.

HOW TO HELP

There are many reproductive health
organizations in need and worthy of your support.

Here is a short list of places to explore if you
are considering a donation.

West Alabama Women's Center
www.action.yellowhammerfund.org/a/wawc

National Latina Institute for Reproductive Health
www.latinainstitute.org

WV FREE
www.wvfree.org

The Mississippi Reproductive Freedom Fund
www.msreprofreedomfund.org/

The Texas Equal Action Fund (TEA Fund)
www.teafund.org

National Network of Abortion Funds
www.abortionfunds.org

Planned Parenthood Federation of America
www.plannedparenthood.org

ACKNOWLEDGMENTS

Every book you've ever held in your hands was born as a result of many hours of labor on the parts of many different people—a long way of saying that every book is, in its own way, an enormous group project. That is certainly true of this anthology, which could only have come into being through the generosity of the thirty-eight different writers, experts, and activists who allowed us to share their words in this collection in the hope that, together, we can build a more just world. To each of those contributors, I offer my enduring gratitude. Your goodwill will indeed move mountains.

Brooke Warner was the very first person I spoke to about this crazy idea of putting together an anthology—fast!—centered on the fight for reproductive freedom after *Roe*, and her belief in this project, and its power to do good, is the main reason you are able to read it today. There are plenty of people who claim to be champions of justice, but Brooke is the real deal; she put her money where her mouth is and helped lift these powerful voices onto the public stage—and I am so grateful to her and the entire team at She Writes Press for their support. So glad the universe put us in each other's orbit.

My thanks also to Amy Ferris, Debra Engle, and the Story Summit team for providing me a teaching home at Her Spirit. Our time together in Santa Fe was life-altering, in all the best ways. Thank you for your belief in me.

To Tanya Bishai, Dianne Williams, Alexandra Ketcham, Jennifer Feeley, Eric and Duffy Mudry, Ted Coons, Liz Yee, Becky van der Bogert, Tiffany Dufu, Gloria Steinem, and V—thank you for being good friends and great people. Your support means the world.

My family is the source of all my inspiration, all my passion, and all that I fight for. Thank you to my mother, Carol Jenkins, for being the ultimate mentor and teacher in this life. To my brother, Mike Hines, for always knowing when to show up with exactly the right treats. To my partner, Jessica Mudry, for holding me up—in all the ways possible—and for your unshakeable loyalty and love. And, most of all, to my children, Avery, Sophie, and Sam: thank you for sharing me with this project. We'll make the world better. I promise.

ABOUT THE EDITOR

ELIZABETH G. HINES is an author and editor whose work has appeared in numerous online publications. Along with her mother, Carol Jenkins, she is the co-author of the best-selling biography, *Black Titan: A. G. Gaston and the Making of a Black American Millionaire*, winner of a 2004 Non-Fiction Book Honor from the American Library Association. Hines holds a BA from Yale College and conducted her graduate studies at Harvard University. She lives in New York City with her family.

@Aftermath_theBook   @BookAftermath

CPSIA information can be obtained
at www.ICGtesting.com
Printed in the USA
JSHW012203290922
31173JS00001B/1

9 781647 426019